16-19 MATHEMATICS

# Locus

Student text and unit guide

The School Mathematics Project

CAMBRIDGE
UNIVERSITY PRESS

**Main authors**          Stan Dolan
                          Andy Hall
                          Thelma Wilson

**Project administrator**  Ann White

Initial work on this unit was carried out by Dave Pratt, Bob Ansell, Sue Burns, Colin Penfold and Peter Wilder.

Artwork by 16–19 Mathematics and Jeff Edwards

Cover illustration by Jeff Edwards

Published by the Press Syndicate of the University of Cambridge
The Pitt Building, Trumpington Street, Cambridge CB2 1RP
40 West 20th Street, New York, NY 10011-4211, USA
10 Stamford Road, Oakleigh, Melbourne 3166, Australia

© Cambridge University Press 1996

First published 1996

Produced by 16–19 Mathematics, Southampton

Printed in Great Britain by Scotprint Ltd., Musselburgh.

ISBN 0  521 56498 0

# Contents and resources

# Introduction to the unit

This unit can be studied independently of other *16–19 Mathematics* units although it would be advantageous for students to have some prior facility at algebra connected with Pythagoras' theorem and completing the square.

This text has been written to facilitate 'supported self-study', and all solutions and commentaries are in this book.

### Chapter 1

Some important themes of this unit are developed in the simple context of equations of circles.

A *locus* is defined as the path of an object moving subject to various *constraints*. The general process of investigating loci is considered, encompassing simple descriptions, mathematical (including algebraic) definitions and rigorous justifications of any assertions.

The particularly important technique of recognising and using the connections between algebraic formulas when curves are translated is also introduced.

### Chapter 2

This chapter focuses on the nature of the constraints. Two particular types of constraint are distinguished, *static* and *dynamic*.

Various forms of these constraints are studied, each of which leads to a locus which is either a straight line or a circle. The final section deals with the proof that one particular locus not only looks like a circle but actually is one.

### Chapter 3

Conics (ellipses, parabolas and hyperbolas) are introduced through the classic use of conic sections. Other definitions are also developed, including the focus-directrix property and the use of sums and differences of distances.

### Chapter 4

This chapter develops the study of conics started in Chapter 3. Here the treatment is much more algebraic and relies upon the ideas of translations covered in Chapter 1.

The equations needed are Cartesian ones, although parametric forms are studied on two extension tasksheets.

**Chapter 5**

In this chapter, the student is encouraged to investigate loci other than those covered in the main text.

Three examples are given, the first two involving the linking of loci. The third example is a study definition of loci if a new type of 'distance' is used, thereby producing 'Taxicab' geometry.

This chapter ends with a list of possible topics for investigation together with a few hints for their study.

# 1 Circles

## 1.1 Fixed points, moving points

The purpose of this book is to study the movement of points in a plane when this movement is **constrained** in a variety of ways. The simple example of the compass illustrates a point, the pencil tip, which moves so that it is always 10 cm from a fixed point.

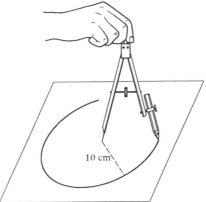

In the diagram below (not to scale), the two points $A$ and $B$ are 10 cm apart and a point $P$ moves so that the area of the triangle $ABP$ is 30 cm².

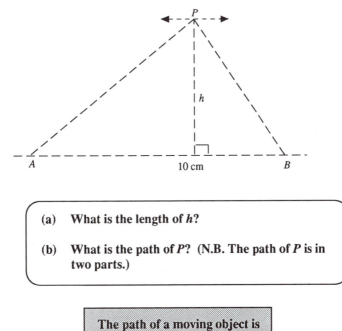

(a) What is the length of $h$?

(b) What is the path of $P$? (N.B. The path of $P$ is in two parts.)

> The path of a moving object is called the *locus* of that object.

When investigating the path of a moving point or its **locus** you will be:

**Describing**:  giving a simple description such as

'the locus of the compass point is a circle.'

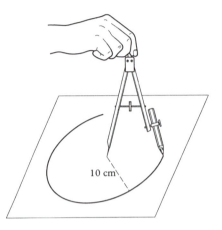

**Defining**:  giving an accepted mathematical definition such as

    (a)    involving constraints:

        'the locus of all points $P$ such that the area of triangle $ABC$ is 30 cm$^2$ where $A$ and $B$ are two fixed points 10 cm apart.'

    (b)    involving algebra:

        'the locus of the points has equation $x^2 + y^2 = 100$.'

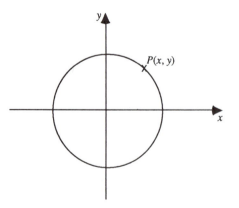

**Justifying**:  giving a convincing reason to justify your description of the locus.

## 1.2    The locus of a circle

The locus generated by considering all of the points which are a fixed distance from a fixed point is easily recognised as fitting our mental picture of a circle.

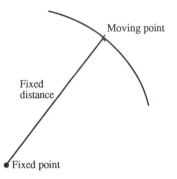

Such a locus can be sketched using pencil and paper. It can also be generated using computer software.

An algebraic definition of the locus can be obtained from the locus definition if the moving point is given coordinates $(x, y)$. For example, let the fixed point be $(0, 0)$ and the distance to the moving point be 300.

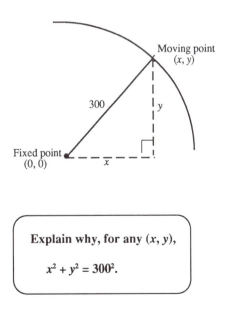

**Explain why, for any $(x, y)$,**

$$x^2 + y^2 = 300^2.$$

This equation gives an **algebraic definition** of the path of the locus and is the equation of a circle with centre $(0, 0)$ and radius 300.

## 1.3 Moving from the origin

The equation of a circle with centre $(0, 0)$ and radius $r$ is

$$x^2 + y^2 = r^2$$

TASKSHEET 1 – *Equations of circles (page 7)*

The image of a circle with centre $(0, 0)$ and radius $r$ when translated $\begin{bmatrix} a \\ b \end{bmatrix}$ is a circle with centre $(a, b)$ and radius $r$. The equation of the new circle is

$$(x - a)^2 + (y - b)^2 = r^2 \qquad ①$$

Expanding the brackets gives

$$x^2 - 2ax + a^2 + y^2 - 2by + b^2 - r^2 = 0$$

$$x^2 - 2ax + y^2 - 2by + C = 0 \qquad ②$$

where $C = a^2 + b^2 - r^2$

Conversely, any equation of the same form as equation ② is the equation of a circle and can be rearranged to give the centre and radius of the circle.

### Example 1

Find the centre and radius of the circle with equation

$$x^2 - 20x + y^2 + 10y - 19 = 0$$

### Solution

$$x^2 - 20x \; + \; y^2 + 10y \; - \; 19 = 0$$

using the method of completing the square

$$(x - 10)^2 - 100 + (y + 5)^2 - 25 - 19 = 0$$

$$\Rightarrow \qquad (x - 10)^2 + (y + 5)^2 - 144 = 0$$

$$(x - 10)^2 + (y + 5)^2 = 144$$

This has the same form as equation ①. So this is a circle with centre $(10, -5)$ and radius 12 units.

> **Explain why the equation**
>
> $$x^2 - 10x + 4xy + y^2 - 8y - 4 = 0$$
>
> **cannot be the equation of a circle.**

## Exercise 1

**1**  Write down the equation of each of these circles in the form

$$(x - a)^2 + (y - b)^2 = r^2$$

(a)  Centre at (0, 4) and radius 5

(b)  Centre at (–3, 2) and radius 3

**2**  Calculate the centre and radius of each of the following circles. Hence write down their equations.

(a)  The points (–6, 0) and (10, 0) are at opposite ends of a diameter.

(b)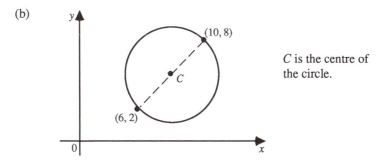

$C$ is the centre of the circle.

**3**  A circle has centre (2, 5) and goes through the point (–3, 17). Work out its radius and hence write down its equation.

**4**  For each of the equations below, state whether it is or is not the equation of a circle. For each circle, find the coordinates of its centre and the radius.

(a)  $x^2 - 4x + y^2 - 6y + 4 = 0$

(b)  $x^2 - 4x + 2xy + y^2 - 4y + 6 = 0$

(c)  $x^2 - 8x + y^2 = 0$

(d)  $x^2 + 4x + y^2 - 4y - 8 = 0$

(e)  $x^2 - 4x - 6y + 3 = 0$

(f)  $x^2 + 12x + y^2 - 4y - 24 = 0$

After working through this chapter you should:

1    understand what is meant by a locus definition;

2    understand and be able to follow the process of

locus definition

↓

mental picture

↓

algebraic definition and justification

3    understand the algebraic effect of moving
the centre of the circle from the origin.

# *Equations of circles*

**1**   A circle with centre (8, 6) has a radius of 5 units.

  (a)   State in terms of $x$ and $y$ the lengths of

    (i)   $CT$

    (ii)  $PT$

  (b)   Explain why

$$CT^2 + PT^2 = 25$$

  (c)   Write down the equation of the circle.

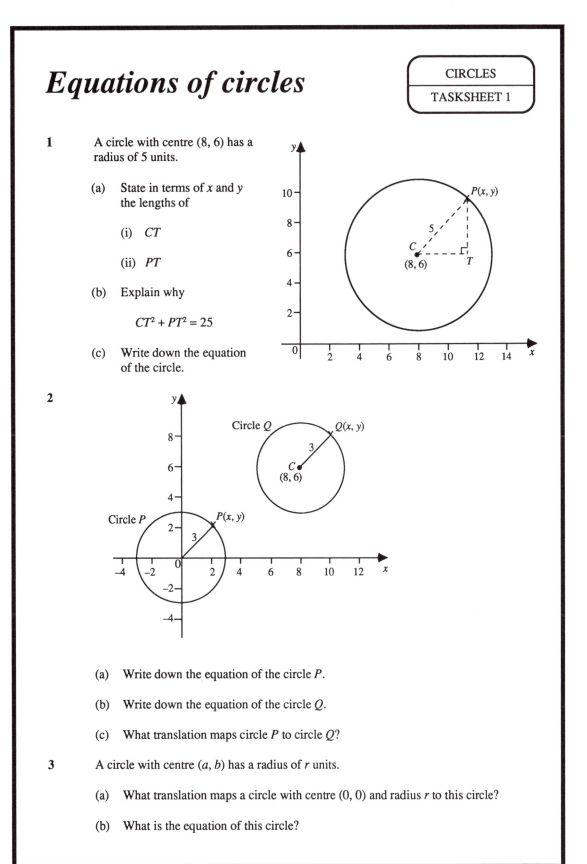

  (a)   Write down the equation of the circle $P$.

  (b)   Write down the equation of the circle $Q$.

  (c)   What translation maps circle $P$ to circle $Q$?

**3**   A circle with centre $(a, b)$ has a radius of $r$ units.

  (a)   What translation maps a circle with centre (0, 0) and radius $r$ to this circle?

  (b)   What is the equation of this circle?

# *Tutorial sheet*

**1**     The point $P$ moves such that $AP = 3$, where $A$ is the fixed point $(2, -1)$.

     (a)    Sketch the locus of $P$.

     (b)    Give the equation of the locus.

**2**     A circle is given by the equation

$$x^2 - 10x + y^2 + 6y + 30 = 0$$

     (a)    Rearrange this equation into the form

$$(x - a)^2 + (y - b)^2 = r^2$$

     (b)    If this circle represents the locus of the moving point $P$, write down a locus definition for $P$.

**3**     Obtain the Cartesian equation of each of the following circles.

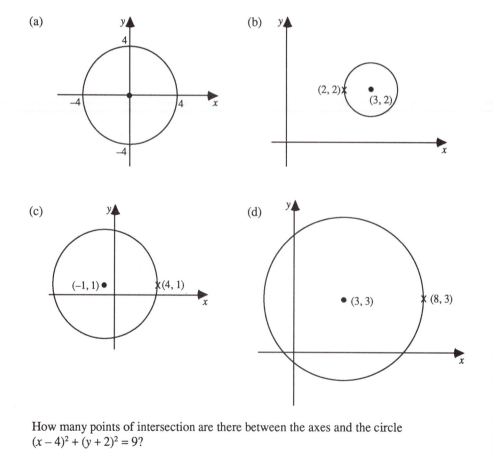

**4**     How many points of intersection are there between the axes and the circle $(x - 4)^2 + (y + 2)^2 = 9$?

# 2   Constraints

## 2.1   Perpendicular bisector

The locus definition given earlier for the circle was based on two constraints.

- A static constraint – the fixed point.

- A dynamic constraint – the fixed distance.

The dynamic constraint was linked to the static constraint. This chapter begins to investigate what happens if the number of static constraints is increased and what happens if the type of dynamic constraint is changed.

TASKSHEET 1 – *The perpendicular bisector (page 18)*

The locus of a point which moves in such a way that its distance from one fixed point is equal to its distance from another fixed point is the perpendicular bisector of the line segment joining the two fixed points.

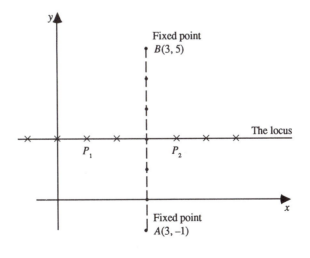

What is the equation of the locus of a point
equidistant from $A(3, -1)$ and $B(3, 5)$?

## 2.2 For any ratio

The locus defined in 2.1 had a dynamic constraint of ratio of lengths 1:1. What happens if another ratio is used?

TASKSHEET 2 – *For any ratio (page 19)*

You should have found that when the ratio is not 1:1 a circle appears to be formed. This can be proved generally by the approach adopted in question 4E of Exercise 1 below. Such circles are known as Apollonius' circles after Apollonius of Perga, a third century BC Greek mathematician famous for his work in geometry.

### Example 1

$O$ is the point $(0, 0)$ and $A$ is the point $(3, 0)$. Find the equation of the locus of $P$ such that $OP = 2AP$.

### Solution

Let $(x, y)$ be a point on the locus.

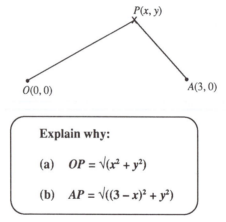

> **Explain why:**
>
> (a)   $OP = \sqrt{(x^2 + y^2)}$
>
> (b)   $AP = \sqrt{((3 - x)^2 + y^2)}$

Let $(x, y)$ be a point on the locus.

$$OP = \sqrt{(x^2 + y^2)} \text{ and } AP = \sqrt{((3 - x)^2 + y^2)}$$
$$\sqrt{(x^2 + y^2)} = 2\sqrt{((3 - x)^2 + y^2)}$$
$$x^2 + y^2 = 4(9 - 6x + x^2 + y^2)$$
$$x^2 + y^2 = 36 - 24x + 4x^2 + 4y^2$$
$$3x^2 + 3y^2 - 24x + 36 = 0$$
$$x^2 + y^2 - 8x + 12 = 0$$
$$(x - 4)^2 - 16 + y^2 + 12 = 0$$
$$(x - 4)^2 + y^2 = 4$$

The locus is a circle with centre $(4, 0)$ and radius 2 units.

**Exercise 1**

**1**

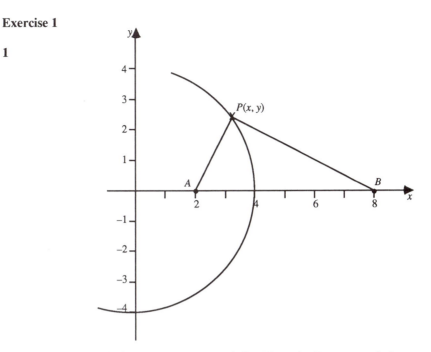

A is the point $(2, 0)$ and B is the point $(8, 0)$. The point P moves such that $BP = 2AP$.

(a) Copy and complete the sketch of the locus of P.

(b) Work out the equation of the locus of P.

(c) Show that the locus is a circle and write down its centre and radius.

**2** O is the point $(0, 0)$ and A is the point $(4, 0)$. The point P moves such that $OP = 3AP$.

(a) Work out the equation of the locus of P.

(b) Describe the locus fully.

**3E** P moves so that it is twice as far from $O(0, 0)$ as it is from $A(a, 0)$. Show that the locus of P is a circle with centre $(\frac{4}{3} a, 0)$ and radius $\frac{2}{3} a$.

**4E** O is the point $(0, 0)$ and A is the point $(a, 0)$. The point P moves such that $PO = \lambda PA$, where $\lambda$ is a constant.

(a) Show that the locus is a circle.

(b) Write down the centre and radius of the circle in terms of $a$ and $\lambda$.

(c) Describe the case when $a = 0$.

(d) Describe the case when $\lambda = 1$.

## 2.3  More equations

Suppose a point $P$ moves in such a way that its distances from two fixed points $A$ and $B$ are such that $AP = \lambda BP$. When $\lambda \neq 1$, there are two points of the locus which are on the line joining the two fixed points.

These two points can be used to find the coordinates of the centre of the circle and its radius. This provides an easy-to-use method for obtaining the equation of the circle.

### Example 2

What is the equation of the locus of the point $P$ if $P$ moves such that $AP = 3BP$ where $A = (1, 0)$ and $B = (9, 0)$?

### Solution

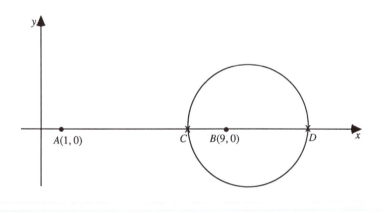

The sketch or mental picture is important and makes it easier to find the equation.

For the coordinates of $C(c, 0)$ and $D(d, 0)$:

$$
\begin{array}{lll}
AC = 3BC & \quad\text{and}\quad & AD = 3BD \\
c - 1 = 3(9 - c) & & d - 1 = 3(d - 9) \\
4c = 28 & & 26 = 2d \\
c = 7 & & 13 = d
\end{array}
$$

So the circle has centre $\left(\dfrac{7 + 13}{2}, 0\right) = (10, 0)$ and radius 3.

Its equation is therefore

$$(x - 10)^2 + y^2 = 9$$

**Exercise 2**

**1**   $A$ is the point $(2, 0)$ and $B$ is the point $(8, 0)$.  The point $P$ moves such that $BP = 2AP$.

   (a)   Work out the coordinates of the two points on the locus which are on the line joining $A$ and $B$.

   (b)   Hence obtain the equation of the locus.

**2**   $A$ is the point $(-2, 0)$ and $B$ is the point $(6, 0)$.  Work out the equation of the locus of $P$ when $P$ moves such that $PB = 3PA$.

**3**   $P$ moves so that is it is 4 times as far from $A(-4, 0)$ as it is from $B(11, 0)$.  Work out the coordinates of the two points on the locus which are on the line joining $A$ and $B$ and hence write down the equation of the locus.

**4**   $A$ is the point $(4, 0)$ and $B$ is the point $(10, 0)$.  Work out the equation of the locus of $P$ where $P$ moves so that its distance from $A$ is half of its distance from $B$.

**5E**

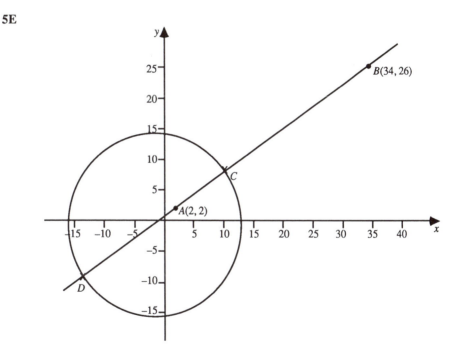

$A$ is the point $(2, 2)$ and $B$ is the point $(34, 26)$.  The point $P$ moves such that $BP = 3AP$.  The locus of $P$ is shown above.

   (a)   Calculate the coordinates of $C$ and $D$.

   (b)   Hence obtain the equation of the locus of $P$.

## 2.4 Fixing an angle

Given two fixed points *A* and *B*, suppose the point *P* moves in such a way that the angle *APB* remains constant.

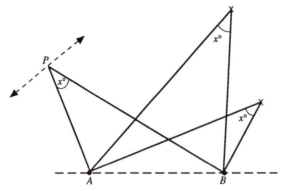

The angle $x°$ is said to be **subtended** by the line segment *AB*.

➡️ TASKSHEET 3 – *Looks like a circle (page 20)*

The mental pictures obtained appear to be those of major or minor arcs of circles, depending on the value of *x*.

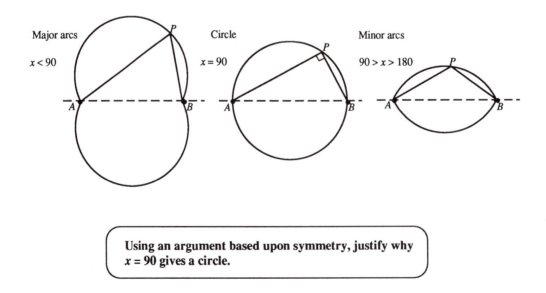

Major arcs    $x < 90$

Circle    $x = 90$

Minor arcs    $90 > x > 180$

> Using an argument based upon symmetry, justify why
> $x = 90$ gives a circle.

## 2.5 Proved and used

The locus given by the moving point $P$ when $A$ and $B$ are two distinct fixed points and the angle $APB$ is fixed appears to be major or minor arcs of a circle, depending on the size of the angle.

TASKSHEET 4E – *The proof (page 21)*

Now that it has been proved that this locus consists of arcs of a circle, you can use this fact to obtain an algebraic definition of the locus.

### Example 3

What is the equation of the locus of the moving point $P$, if angle $APB = 60°$ where $A$ and $B$ are the points with coordinates $(0, 0)$ and $(8, 0)$ respectively?

### Solution

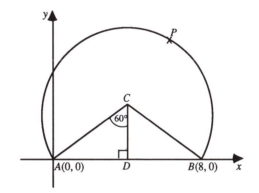

The centre $C$ of the circle is the point on the perpendicular bisector of $AB$ such that angle $ACB$ is $120°$.

Using triangle $ACD$

$$\tan 60° = \frac{4}{CD}$$

$$\Rightarrow CD = 2.31$$

$$\Rightarrow C \text{ is the point } (4, 2.31).$$

$$AC = \sqrt{(4^2 + 2.31^2)}$$

$$= 4.62$$

The locus is part of the circle with equation $(x - 4)^2 + (y - 2.31)^2 \approx 21.3$ and part of the circle $(x - 4)^2 + (y + 2.31)^2 \approx 21.3$.

**Exercise 3**

**1**

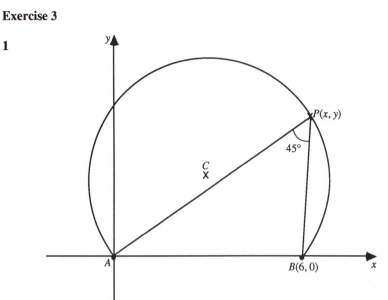

(a)   What is the angle *ACB*?

(b)   What are the coordinates of *C*, the centre of the circle?

(c)   What is the radius of the circle?

(d)   What is the equation of the part of the locus of the moving point *P* shown above?

**2**   What are the equations of the two parts of the locus of the moving point *P* if angle *APB* $= 70°$, where *A* and *B* are the points with coordinates $(-10, 0)$ and $(4, 0)$ respectively?

**3**   *A* is the point $(4, 0)$, *B* is the point $(12, 0)$ and *P* is the moving point such that *APB* $= 90°$. What is the equation of the locus of *P*?

**4E**   (a)   What is the angle *ACB*?

(b)   What are the coordinates of *C*, the centre of the circle?

(c)   What is the radius of the circle?

(d)   What is the equation of the locus of the moving point *P*?

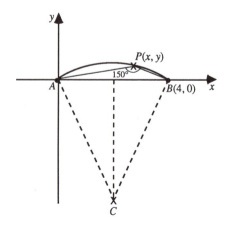

After working through this chapter you should:

1  understand the need for and what is meant by 'proof';

2  be able to recognise and obtain algebraic definitions of the loci given by

(a)  the moving point $P$ where $AP = \lambda BP$,

(b)  the moving point $P$ where the angle $APB = \theta$.

In each case $A$ and $B$ are two distinct fixed points.

# The perpendicular bisector

**Locus definition**

The two points $A$ and $B$ are distinct fixed points. The point $P$ moves so that $AP = PB$.

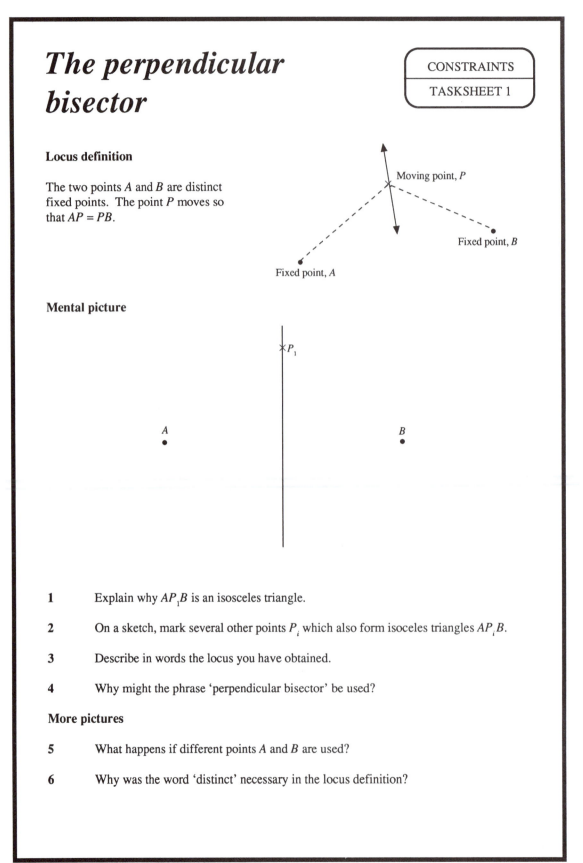

Moving point, $P$

Fixed point, $B$

Fixed point, $A$

**Mental picture**

$\times P_1$

$A$

$B$

1    Explain why $AP_1B$ is an isosceles triangle.

2    On a sketch, mark several other points $P_i$ which also form isoceles triangles $AP_iB$.

3    Describe in words the locus you have obtained.

4    Why might the phrase 'perpendicular bisector' be used?

**More pictures**

5    What happens if different points $A$ and $B$ are used?

6    Why was the word 'distinct' necessary in the locus definition?

# *For any ratio*

**Locus definition**

The two distinct points $A$ and $B$ are fixed and $P$ moves so that the ratio of the lengths $AP$ to $BP$ is $\lambda$, i.e. $AP = \lambda BP$.

**Mental pictures**

To find the family of loci defined by the above statement, a structured investigation is needed.

**1**

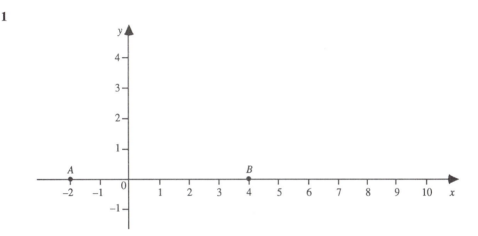

A is the point $(-2, 0)$ and $B$ is the point $(4, 0)$. The point $P$ moves so that $AP = 2BP$.

On a copy of the axes

(a) Draw a circle of radius 3 centre $B$ and a circle of radius 6 centre $A$. Label the points of intersection $P_1$ and $P_2$.

(b) Repeat this with other pairs of circles of radii $r$ and $2r$ respectively, obtaining further points $P_i$. Describe the locus in words.

**2** Move $B$ to $(7, 0)$ but keep $AP = 2BP$. What is the effect?

**3** Keep $A$ and $B$ at $(-2, 0)$ and $(4, 0)$ and change the ratio to give $AP = \frac{1}{2} BP$. What is the locus now obtained?

**4** A group exercise: using any $A$ and $B$ and any values for $\lambda$, describe the family of loci obtained. Remember that $\lambda = 1$ is a special case.

# *Looks like a circle*

**Locus definition**

The two points $A$ and $B$ are distinct fixed points. The point $P$ moves so that the angle $APB$ is constant.

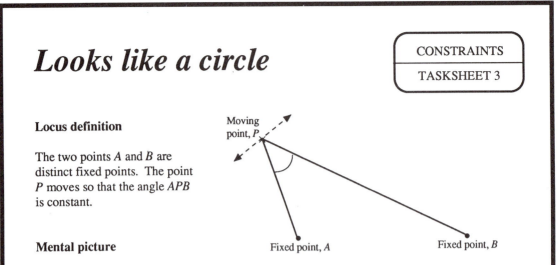

**Mental picture**

You will need a number of copies of Datasheet 1 – *Fixed angle loci*. [Alternatively, a set square can be used for an angle of 30°, 60° or 90°.]

**1** From the bottom half of the datasheet cut out the 40° wedge.

**2** (a) Position the wedge so that $A$ and $B$ lie on its edges. Mark the position of point $P_1$.

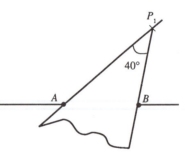

(b) Repeat this for other positions of the wedge.

(c) Join up all the positions of $P_i$ to complete the locus.

(d) State, with reasons, what you think the locus is that you have obtained.

**3** (a) Obtain loci using the other wedges. Are they similar?

(b) What is special about the locus if the angle is 90°?

(c) Are there any other special cases (some of which may seem trivial)?

**4** You may assume that the loci you have obtained are circular. For any one of these loci:

(a) Estimate the position of $Q$, the centre of the circle.

(b) Form an hypothesis about the relationship between the angles $APB$ and $AQB$.

(c) Attempt to justify your hypothesis.

# *The proof*

Let $P$ be a point such that angle $APB$ is the fixed value $\theta$, where $A$ and $B$ are fixed points.

A useful geometrical construction is to define $C$ to be the point on the perpendicular bisector of $AB$ such that angle $ACB = 2\theta$ and to define $Q$ to be the point on $AP$ such that $CQ = CA = CB$.

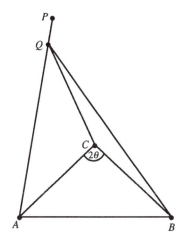

Let angle $CAQ = a$ and let angle $CBQ = b$. Then

$$\text{angle } ACQ = 180 - 2a \quad \text{①}$$
$$\text{angle } BCQ = 180 - 2b \quad \text{②}$$

So
$$(180 - 2a) + (180 - 2b) + 2\theta = 360 \quad \text{③}$$
$$\Rightarrow \quad \theta = a + b \quad \text{④}$$

Then angle $AQB$ is $\theta$ and therefore $Q$ and $P$ are the same point. This proves that $P$ lies on a circle centre $C$, radius $CA$.

1    Explain equation ①.

2    Explain how equations ① and ② lead to equation ③ and hence to equation ④.

3    Why can it be deduced that 'angle $AQB$ is $\theta$'?

4    Justify the conclusion that 'therefore $Q$ and $P$ are the same point'.

5    Strictly speaking, the above proof is only valid for $0° < \theta < 90°$. Where was this restriction relevant?

6    In the above proof, the diagram was drawn with $C$ inside triangle $AQB$. Write out the proof for the case where $C$ is outside triangle $AQB$.

1   The point $P$ moves such that $AP = \lambda PB$ when $A$ and $B$ are two distinct fixed points.

(a)   Categorise the loci obtained for $0 \le \lambda < 2$.

(b)   When $A = (4, 0)$ and $B = (-5, 0)$, obtain the equation of the locus for $\lambda = 2$.

2

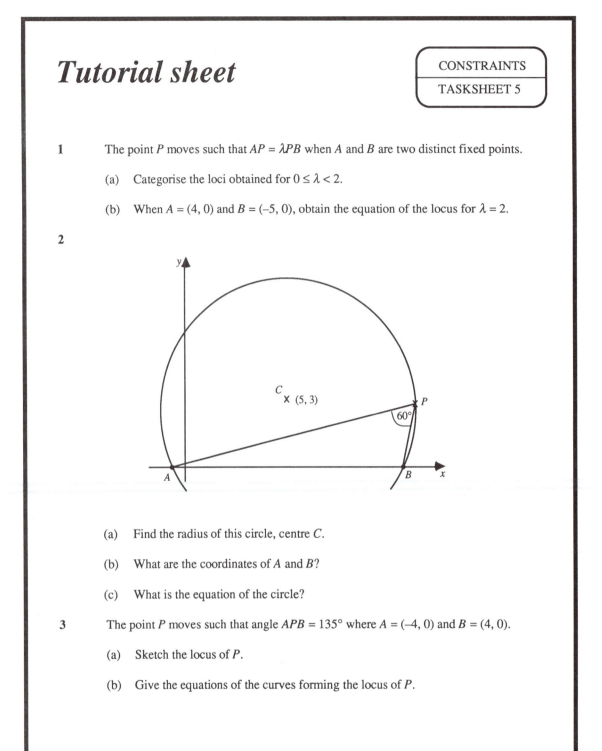

(a)   Find the radius of this circle, centre $C$.

(b)   What are the coordinates of $A$ and $B$?

(c)   What is the equation of the circle?

3   The point $P$ moves such that angle $APB = 135°$ where $A = (-4, 0)$ and $B = (4, 0)$.

(a)   Sketch the locus of $P$.

(b)   Give the equations of the curves forming the locus of $P$.

# 3 Conics

## 3.1 Cutting a cone

When an object is cut by a knife a section is obtained. If the plane of the cut is parallel to the end of the object, then the section is called a **cross-section**.

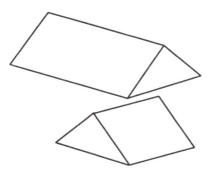

For a triangular prism, it is clear that the cross-section is a triangle.

> **What is the cross-section of a cone?**

This chapter studies all the sections of a cone. These constitute an important family of shapes and curves which have been given the name **conics**.

 TASKSHEET 1 – *Imagination or reality? (page 30)*

The tasksheet appeared to show four different conics. In fact there are only three.

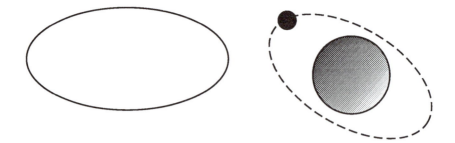

The **ellipse** occurs in many situations. For example, the Moon moves on an elliptical path around the Earth. The circle is a special case of an ellipse; it is an ellipse which is as wide as it is long.

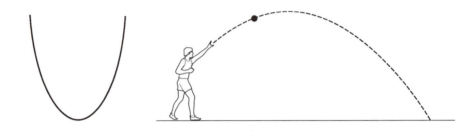

The **parabola** also occurs in many situations, such as the path of a projectile. The path of the shot above can be reasonably modelled by a parabola.

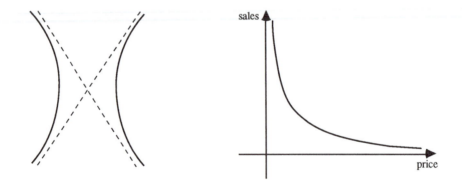

The **hyperbola**, which has two asymptotes, is most frequently seen describing the values of two inversely proportional quantities. As one goes up the other goes down.

> **Describe some other situations in which these curves are involved.**

The next sections of this chapter look for locus definitions of the conics using static and dynamic constraints.

## 3.2    Focus and directrix

To obtain any of the conics from a moving point $P$, one family of locus definitions is based on the following.

**Static constraints**

(a)    A fixed point $A$ which is known as the **focus**

(b)    A fixed line known as the **directrix**

**Dynamic constraints**

The ratio of the distance $AP$ to the shortest distance of $P$ from the directrix is fixed and is called $e$.

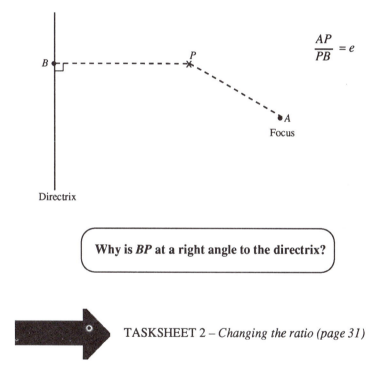

$$\frac{AP}{PB} = e$$

Why is *BP* at a right angle to the directrix?

TASKSHEET 2 – *Changing the ratio (page 31)*

The tasksheet did, in fact, show that all three types of conic can be generated depending on the value, $e$, of the ratio:

For    $0 < e < 1$,    the locus is an ellipse.

For    $e = 1$,    the locus is a parabola.

For    $e > 1$,    the locus is a hyperbola.

The important value $e$ is called the **eccentricity** of the conic.

25

In the following exercise, you are asked to produce **sketches** of various conics. If you find it hard to visualise what is happening, you may find it helpful to make more accurate drawings of the loci using the method described in Tasksheet 2.

**Exercise 1**

1   Point $P$ moves so that it is twice as far from the line $x = 6$ as it is from the origin.

   (a)   What will be the shape of the locus?

   (b)   Calculate the coordinates of the two points on the locus which lie on the $x$-axis.

   (c)   Sketch the locus, by first marking on your sketch the points you calculated in (b) and then visualising three or four more positions on the locus.

2   Repeat question 1 for the locus of a point which moves so that it is twice as far from the origin as it is from the line $x = 6$.

3

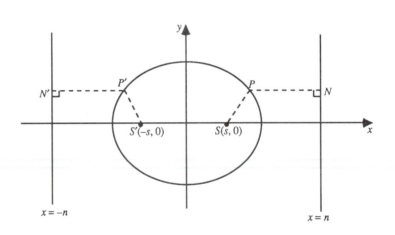

'The point $P$ moves so that it is twice as far from the line $x = n$ as it is from the point $S$'.

'The point $P'$ moves so that it is twice as far from the line $x = -n$ as it is from the point $S''$.

Using an argument based upon symmetry, justify why these two definitions give the same locus.

**4**    Sketch each of the loci described in the table below.

|      | Focus    | Directrix | Eccentricity |
|------|----------|-----------|--------------|
| (a)  | $(-6, 0)$ | $x = 6$   | $\frac{1}{3}$ |
| (b)  | $(-6, 0)$ | $x = 6$   | $3$ |
| (c)  | $(-6, 0)$ | $x = 6$   | $1$ |
| (d)  | $(0, 0)$ | $x = -5$  | $\frac{2}{3}$ |
| (e)  | $(0, 0)$ | $x = 5$   | $1\frac{1}{2}$ |

**5**    Four of the loci in question 4 could have been described with reference to a different focus and directrix.

(a)    Which loci are these?

(b)    Give the alternative positions of the focus and directrix in each case.

## 3.3 Pins and string

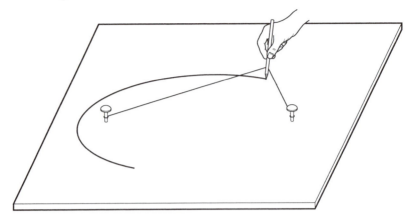

Imagine a piece of string pinned to a table at its two ends, and a pencil moving so that the string is kept at full stretch at all times.

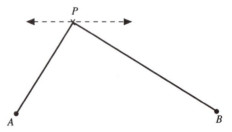

(a) What conic section does this produce?

(b) Give a locus definition based on this idea.

 TASKSHEET 3 – *Sums and differences (page 33)*

Let *A* and *B* be two distinct fixed points.

- If *AP* + *PB* is constant then the locus of *P* is an ellipse.

- If │ *AP* – *PB* │ is constant then the locus of *P* is a hyperbola.

After working through this chapter you should:

1   recognise the three different conic sections

    (a)    ellipse,

    (b)    parabola,

    (c)    hyperbola;

2   understand the locus definitions of conics based on the three terms

    (a)    focus,

    (b)    directrix,

    (c)    eccentricity;

3   be aware of other locus definitions of conics;

4   be able to deduce which conic section is given by a locus definition.

# *Imagination or reality?*

Note: The aim of this tasksheet is to show approximately the sorts of curves given by this construction and their subsequent name 'the conics'.

For any three-dimensional object, the movement, construction or alteration of it can pose difficulties of visualisation. Sometimes one can 'see' or visualise the result. Often, however, it seems impossible unless you can actually do it 'for real'. If a more accurate visualisation is required it is possible to purchase some very good 3D models, or perhaps make some yourself.

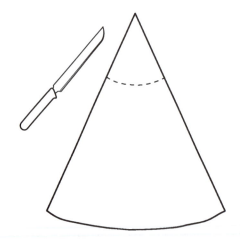

For the cone, a horizontal cut will clearly produce a circle, larger or smaller, depending how high or low the cut is made. This is easy to 'see'.

Other cuts can be made.

1    (a)    For a sloping cut, what section will be made?

     (b)    Sketch your solution.

     You might 'see' this or be able to talk it through with others. You may find it clearer if you make a small cone and cut it.

2    Two other types of cut can be made.

     (a)    What are they?

     (b)    For each cut, sketch the section obtained.

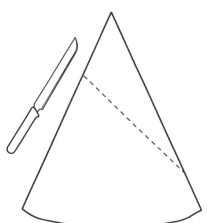

# *Changing the ratio*

**Locus definition**

$\frac{AP}{PB} = e$, where $A$ is the focus and $PB$ is the perpendicular to the directrix.

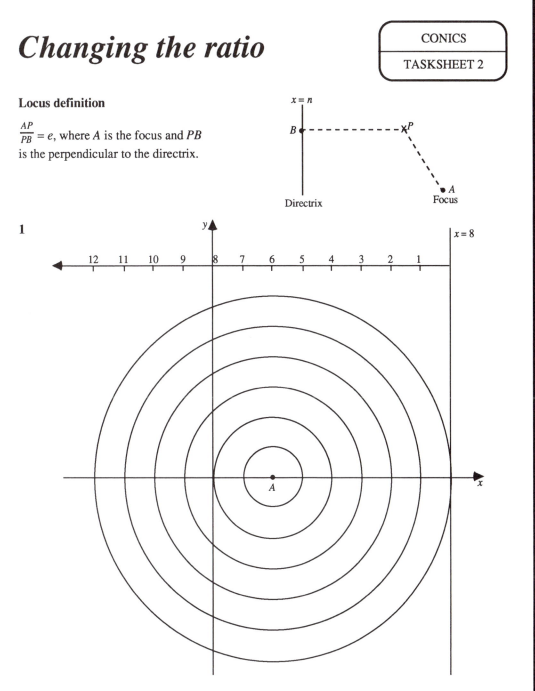

**1**

The focus $A$ is the point $(2, 0)$ and the directrix is the line $x = 8$. The point $P$ moves so that $\frac{AP}{PB} = \frac{1}{2}$.

(a)  Explain why $P_1(4, 0)$ and $P_2(-4, 0)$ are two points on the locus.

(b)  Copy the diagram and find various points $P_i$ on the circles such that $AP_i$ is half the distance of $P_i$ from the directrix. Hence obtain the locus of the moving point $P$.

(continued)

**2**     The locus obtained in question 1 is one of the three conic sections. By elimination it is possible to deduce which it must be.

(a)   Does the locus appear to be closed?

(b)   Is the locus continuous?

(c)   Is the locus in two separate parts?

(d)   What sort of conic is the locus?

**3**

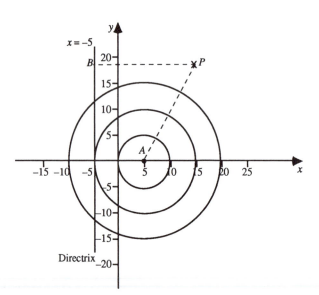

The focus $A$ is the point $(5, 0)$ and the directrix is the line $x = -5$. The point $P$ moves so that $AP = PB$, (i.e. $e = 1$). Using a copy of the above diagram on graph paper, find various points $P_i$ on the circles such that $AP_i$ equals the distance of $P_i$ from the directrix. Hence obtain and describe in words the locus of the moving point $P$. (You will probably need to draw more circles.)

**4**     The focus $A$ is the point $(8, 0)$ and the directrix is the line $x = 2$. The point $P$ moves so that $AP = 2PB$ (i.e. $e = 2$). Draw a suitable diagram on graph paper and hence obtain the locus of the moving point $P$.

**5**     **Group activity**

(a)   Investigate the loci obtained when other values are used for the ratio $e$.

(b)   Classify the loci obtained for different values of $e$.

(c)   Write out a locus definition for

(i)    an ellipse

(ii)   a parabola

(iii)  a hyperbola

# *Sums and differences*

You will need to use a compass for this tasksheet.
In all the questions $A$ and $B$ are two distinct points
as shown.

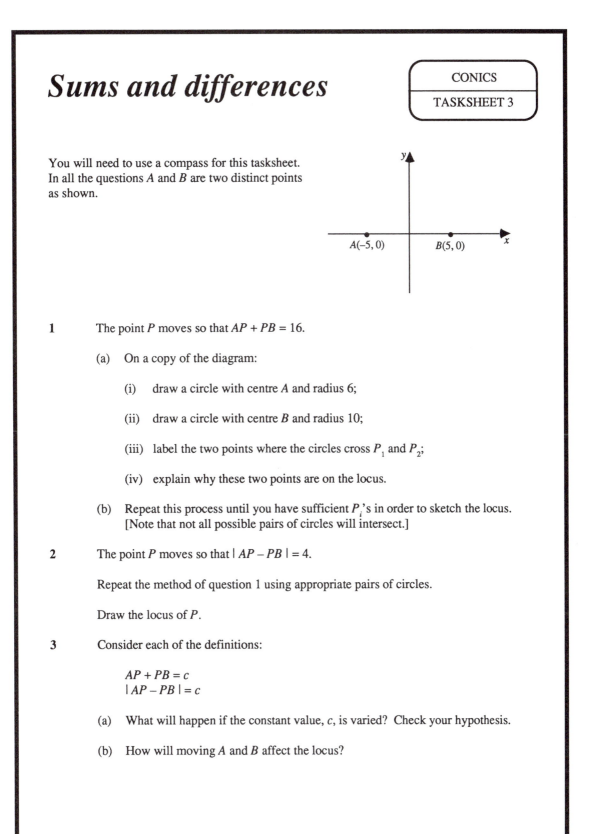

1    The point $P$ moves so that $AP + PB = 16$.

    (a)   On a copy of the diagram:

        (i)    draw a circle with centre $A$ and radius 6;

        (ii)   draw a circle with centre $B$ and radius 10;

        (iii)  label the two points where the circles cross $P_1$ and $P_2$;

        (iv)  explain why these two points are on the locus.

    (b)   Repeat this process until you have sufficient $P_i$'s in order to sketch the locus.
        [Note that not all possible pairs of circles will intersect.]

2    The point $P$ moves so that $|\, AP - PB \,| = 4$.

    Repeat the method of question 1 using appropriate pairs of circles.

    Draw the locus of $P$.

3    Consider each of the definitions:

    $$AP + PB = c$$
    $$|\, AP - PB \,| = c$$

    (a)   What will happen if the constant value, $c$, is varied?  Check your hypothesis.

    (b)   How will moving $A$ and $B$ affect the locus?

# Tutorial sheet

**1**

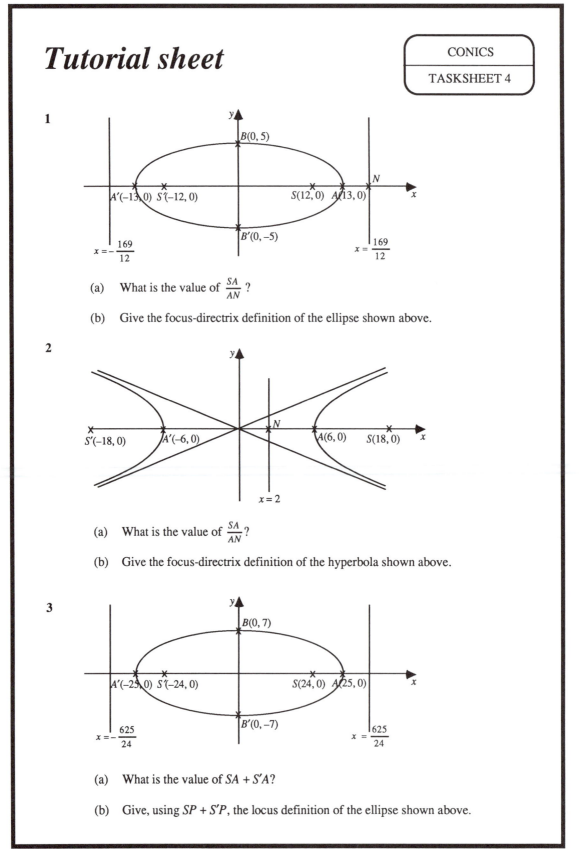

(a)   What is the value of $\dfrac{SA}{AN}$ ?

(b)   Give the focus-directrix definition of the ellipse shown above.

**2**

(a)   What is the value of $\dfrac{SA}{AN}$ ?

(b)   Give the focus-directrix definition of the hyperbola shown above.

**3**

(a)   What is the value of $SA + S'A$?

(b)   Give, using $SP + S'P$, the locus definition of the ellipse shown above.

# 4 Algebra

## 4.1 Parabolas

Once the geometric representation of a conic section is known then, as shown in earlier chapters, algebra can be used to justify the description of a locus.

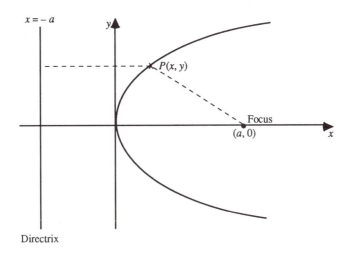

For the parabola shown, let $P$ have coordinates $(x, y)$, then

$$x + a = \sqrt{\left((a-x)^2 + y^2\right)} \qquad \text{①}$$

$$(x + a)^2 = a^2 - 2ax + x^2 + y^2$$

$$x^2 + 2ax + a^2 - a^2 + 2ax - x^2 = y^2$$

$$4ax = y^2$$

---

**(a)** **Explain line ①.**

**(b)** **'Because $a$ is in the equation the parabola obtained is dependent on the value of $a$.'**

**What does this statement mean?**

---

The equation $y^2 = 4ax$ is the general equation of a parabola passing through the origin and having the $x$-axis as its axis of symmetry. To deal with other parabolas it is important to understand how the equation of a curve is affected by translations (see Chapter 1).

**Example 1**

Describe in words the locus which has equation $80(x - 20) = (y - 10)^2$.

**Solution**

Rewriting the equation as $\qquad 4 \times 20 \times (x - 20) = (y - 10)^2$

and comparing to $\qquad 4 \times a \times x = y^2$

shows that $a$ is 20, $x$ is replaced by $(x - 20)$ and $y$ is replaced by $(y - 10)$.

For a parabola symmetrical about the $x$-axis and passing through the origin, and with $a = 20$, the focus is at $(20, 0)$ and the directrix is $x = -20$.

The replacements for $x$ and $y$ mean that the object is translated $\begin{bmatrix} 20 \\ 10 \end{bmatrix}$ from the origin and the directrix is now the $y$-axis.

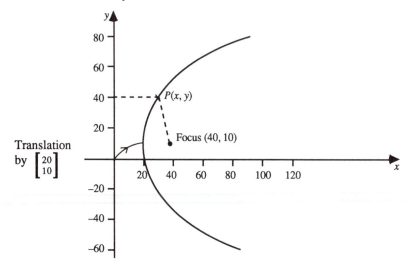

In order to confirm that the locus drawn and described in words above is correct, consider a general point $P(x, y)$.

$$x = \sqrt{((40 - x)^2 + (y - 10)^2)}$$

$$x^2 = 1600 - 80x + x^2 + (y - 10)^2$$

$$80x - 1600 = (y - 10)^2$$

$$80(x - 20) = (y - 10)^2$$

The equation is often left in this form with the $(y - 10)^2$ not multiplied out because it is then straightforward to describe the locus in words.

TASKSHEET 1E – *Parameters (page 48)*

36

## Exercise 1

**1** Consider the curve with equation $y^2 = 200(x - 50)$.

    (a) Explain why the curve is symmetrical about the $x$-axis.

    (b) Use the equation to find the point where the curve will cross the $x$-axis.

    (c) What are the positions of the focus and directrix of the curve?

**2**

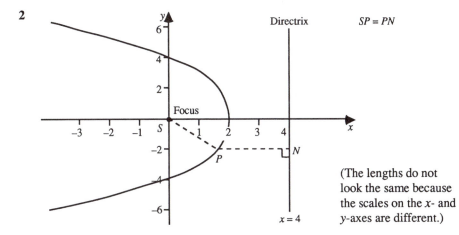

(The lengths do not look the same because the scales on the $x$- and $y$-axes are different.)

A point $P$ moves so that its distance from the origin is equal to its shortest distance from the line $x = 4$. Show that the locus of $P$ has the equation

$$y^2 = 16 - 8x$$

**3** A point $P$ moves so that its distance from the focus at the origin is equal to its shortest distance from the directrix, $x = -4$. Draw a sketch to show this and work out the equation of the locus of $P$.

**4** A point $P$ moves so that its distance from the focus at $A(-4, 0)$ is equal to its distance from the directrix $x = 4$. Draw a sketch to show this and work out the equation of the locus of $P$.

**5** Work out the equation of the locus of $P$ for the directrix $y = -a$ and the focus $(0, a)$, where $P$ moves so that its distance is equal to the distance from the directrix.

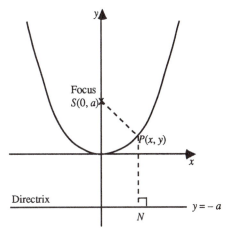

## 4.2 Equations

For the parabola, you have seen the relationship between the shape of the curve and its equation. This section investigates equations for ellipses and hyperbolas.

TASKSHEET 2 – *a and b (page 49)*

For an equation of the form $\dfrac{x^2}{a^2} + \dfrac{y^2}{b^2} = 1$ the curve will be an ellipse. The ellipse will intersect the axes at $(\pm a, 0)$, $(0, \pm b)$.

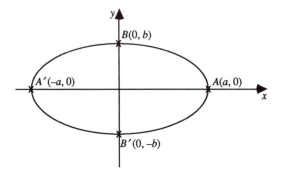

For an equation of the form $\dfrac{x^2}{a^2} - \dfrac{y^2}{b^2} = 1$ the curve will be a hyperbola. The hyperbola will intersect the $x$-axis at $(\pm a, 0)$ and will have asymptotes with equations $y = \pm \dfrac{b}{a}\, x$.

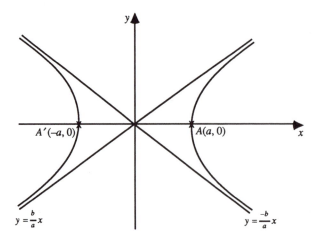

## Example 2

The ellipse shown below has eccentricty $\frac{1}{2}$ , focus $(s, 0)$ and directrix $x = d$.

(a)  By considering the points $A$ and $A'$, work out the values of $s$ and $d$.

(b)  Work out the exact value of $b$.

(c)  Find the equation of the ellipse.

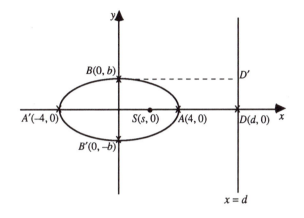

## Solution

(a)  $SA = \frac{1}{2} AD \quad \Rightarrow \quad 4 - s = \frac{1}{2}(d - 4)$

$SA' = \frac{1}{2} A'D \quad \Rightarrow \quad 4 + s = \frac{1}{2}(d + 4)$

So: $4 - s = \frac{1}{2} d - 2 \qquad$ ①

$4 + s = \frac{1}{2} d + 2 \qquad$ ②

① + ② gives $8 = d$

② − ① gives $2s = 4$

$s = 2$ and $d = 8$

(b)  $SB = \frac{1}{2} BD' \qquad \sqrt{(b^2 + 2^2)} = \frac{1}{2} d = 4$

$b^2 + 4 = 16$, so $b = \sqrt{12}$

(c)  $a = 4, b = \sqrt{12}$, so $\dfrac{x^2}{16} + \dfrac{y^2}{12} = 1$

**Why has the answer to (b) been left in surd form?**

**Exercise 2**

**1**   The ellipse shown has eccentricity $e$, focus $S$ and directrix $x = n$.

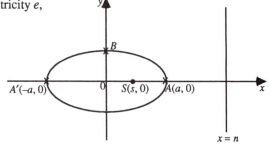

(a)   By considering the point $A$, explain why $a - s = en - ea$. Similarly, explain why $a + s = en + ea$.

(b)   Use the equations in (a) to find an expression for $ae$.

(c)   If the eccentricity is 0.25 and $s = 5$, find the values of $a$ and $n$.

(d)   By considering the point $B$, find the value of $b$ and so write down the equation of the ellipse in (c).

**2**   An ellipse intersects the $x$-axis at the points $A(12, 0)$ and $A'(-12, 0)$ and the $y$-axis at the points $B(0, b)$ and $B'(0, -b)$. It has eccentricity $\frac{1}{3}$. The focus is at $(s, 0)$ and the directrix is $x = d$.

(a)   Sketch the ellipse, choosing reasonable positions for $(s, 0)$ and $(d, 0)$.

(b)   By using the fact that each of the points $A$ and $A'$ are $\frac{1}{3}$ as far from $(s, 0)$ as they are from $x = d$, work out the values of $s$ and $d$.

(c)   By considering the point $B$ or $B'$ calculate the exact value of $b$.

(d)   Write down the equation of the ellipse.

**3**

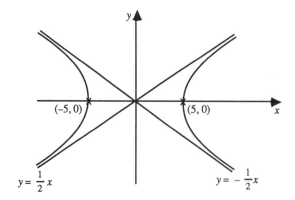

(a)   Obtain the values of $a$ and $b$ so that you can write down the equation of this hyperbola in the form $\frac{x^2}{a^2} - \frac{y^2}{b^2} = 1$.

(b)   What is the angle between the asymptote $y = \frac{1}{2}x$ and the $x$-axis?

## 4.3 Ellipses

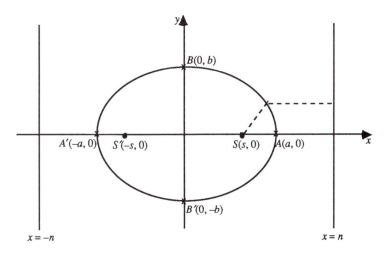

For the ellipse shown above the focus is at $S$, the directrix is $x = n$ and the eccentricity is $e$.

> **Why could the definition of this ellipse also be based on $S'$, $x = -n$ and $e$?**

Given that the horizontal axis from $A$ to $A'$ is the longest axis of this ellipse, it is known as the major axis and is of length $2a$. The vertical axis from $B$ to $B'$ is then known as the minor axis and is of length $2b$.

TASKSHEET 3 – *Facts and formulas (page 50)*

From the tasksheet it can be seen that the expression $b^2 = a^2(1 - e^2)$ connects the major and minor axes. Furthermore, the equations $s = ae$ and $n = \dfrac{a}{e}$ connect the focus, directrix and values of $a$ and $e$. The ellipse is therefore dependent on the values of $a$ and $e$ only.

> **(a) Explain how the ellipse varies as $a$ and $e$ are varied.**
>
> **(b) What is obtained for the extreme values of $e$, which are 0 and 1?**

41

The dependence on $a$ and $e$ is demonstrated for the 'pins and string' fixed distance locus definition. Having chosen $a$ and $e$, the position of the pins is $2ae$ apart and the length of string is $2a$.

**Example 3**

A piece of string 10 units long is attached to two pins 6 units apart. A pencil is then used to keep the string taut. What locus will the pencil draw as it moves, keeping the string taut at all times?

**Solution**

The pins are placed at $S$ and $S'$, 6 units apart as shown. The length of string is therefore

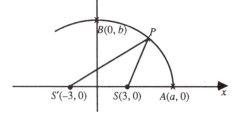

$10 = SA + S'A = (a - 3) + (a + 3) = 2a.$

Then $A = (5, 0)$ and $A' = (-5, 0)$

Also, $s = ae \Rightarrow 3 = 5e \Rightarrow e = \dfrac{3}{5}$

$\quad n = \dfrac{a}{e} \Rightarrow n = \dfrac{25}{3}$

$\quad b = a\sqrt{(1 - e^2)} \Rightarrow b = 4$

The ellipse has equation

$$\frac{x^2}{25} + \frac{y^2}{16} = 1$$

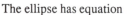

TASKSHEET 4E – *Parametric form (page 52)*

**Exercise 3**

1   $P$ is the moving point such that for the fixed points $C(-5, 0)$ and $D(5, 0)$
$PC + PD = 16$.

  (a)  Sketch the ellipse formed by the locus of $P$.

  (b)  Calculate the lengths of the major and minor axes.

  (c)  What is the eccentricity?

  (d)  Calculate the equations of the two possible directrices.

  (e)  What is the equation of the ellipse?

2   The ellipse shown below has its focus at $(3, 0)$ and eccentricity $\frac{3}{5}$ . Work out the
equation of the directrix and the coordinates of $B$ and $B'$.  Hence write down the
equation of the ellipse.

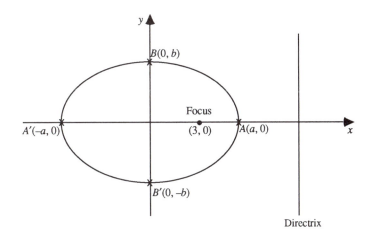

3   The ellipse $\dfrac{x^2}{a^2} + \dfrac{y^2}{b^2} = 1$ has a focus at $(s, 0)$ and directrix $x = n$.

  (a)  By considering the points $(a, 0)$ and $(-a, 0)$, obtain two equations
connecting $a$, $e$, $s$ and $n$.

  (b)  By considering one of the points $(b, 0)$ or $(-b, 0)$, obtain an expression for
$b^2$ in terms of $e$, $n$ and $s$.

  (c)  Show how the answers to parts (b) and (c) lead to the equation
$b^2 = a^2 (1 - e^2)$.

## 4.4 Hyperbolas

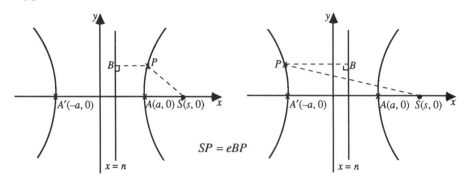

$$SP = eBP$$

When $P$ reaches $A$

$$s - a = e(a - n)$$
$$s - a = ea - en \qquad ①$$

When $P$ reaches $A'$

$$s + a = e(a + n)$$
$$s + a = ea + en \qquad ②$$

$$s = ae \qquad ① + ②$$
$$a = en \qquad ② - ①$$

In general,

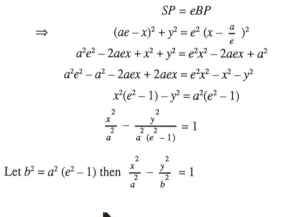

$$SP = eBP$$

$$\Rightarrow \qquad (ae - x)^2 + y^2 = e^2 \left(x - \frac{a}{e}\right)^2$$

$$a^2e^2 - 2aex + x^2 + y^2 = e^2x^2 - 2aex + a^2$$

$$a^2e^2 - a^2 - 2aex + 2aex = e^2x^2 - x^2 - y^2$$

$$x^2(e^2 - 1) - y^2 = a^2(e^2 - 1)$$

$$\frac{x^2}{a^2} - \frac{y^2}{a^2(e^2 - 1)} = 1$$

Let $b^2 = a^2(e^2 - 1)$ then $\dfrac{x^2}{a^2} - \dfrac{y^2}{b^2} = 1$

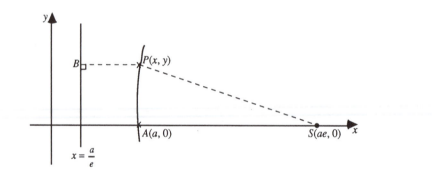

TASKSHEET 5 – *Asymptotes (page 53)*

44

The general equations for the ellipse and hyperbola are very similar, as are the other associated facts and formulas. For the hyperbola the general equation is

$$\frac{x^2}{a^2} - \frac{y^2}{b^2} = 1$$

with asymptotes at $y = \frac{b}{a} x$ and $y = -\frac{b}{a} x$.

It can also be stated that $b^2 = a^2(e^2 - 1)$, $s = ae$ and $n = \frac{a}{e}$, thus connecting the focus, directrix and values of $a$ and $e$. All these show that the hyperbola is dependent on the values of $a$ and $e$ only.

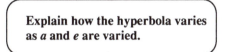

**Explain how the hyperbola varies as *a* and *e* are varied.**

**Example 4**

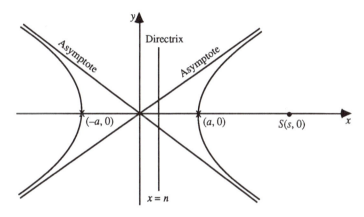

A hyperbola has a focus at the point $(6, 0)$ and an eccentricity of 3.

(a)  Where is the directrix?

(b)  What is the equation of the hyperbola?

(c)  What are the equations of the asymptotes?

**Solution**

(a)  Using  $s = ae \Rightarrow 6 = 3a \Rightarrow a = 2$
     using  $n = \frac{a}{e} \Rightarrow n = \frac{2}{3}$
          The directrix is $x = \frac{2}{3}$.

(b)  Using  $b^2 = a^2 (e^2 - 1) \Rightarrow b^2 = 4(9 - 1)$
          The equation is $\frac{x^2}{4} - \frac{y^2}{32} = 1$.

(c)  Using  $y = \pm \frac{b}{a} x$
          The asymptotes are $y = \sqrt{8}x$ and $y = -\sqrt{8}x$.

45

**1**

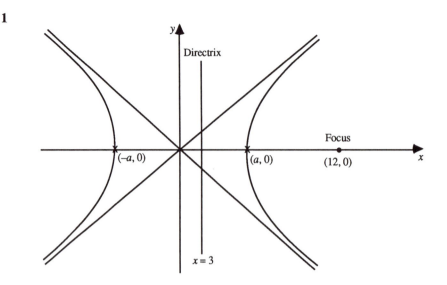

For the hyperbola shown above:

(a)   calculate the eccentricity $e$ and the value of $a$;

(b)   write down the equation of the hyperbola.

**2**   A hyperbola is symmetrical about the $x$- and $y$-axes, and has eccentricity 4 and a directrix at $x = \dfrac{1}{2}$ .

(a)   Where is the focus?

(b)   Obtain the equation of the hyperbola.

**3**   A hyperbola is symmetrical about the $x$- and $y$-axes, and has eccentricity $\sqrt{2}$ and focus at $(s, 0)$. Show that the asymptotes have gradients $\pm 1$.

**4**   A hyperbola has equation

$$\frac{x^2}{25} - \frac{y^2}{39} = 1$$

(a)   Calculate the coordinates of the intercepts with the $x$-axis.

(b)   Calculate the eccentricity.

(c)   Calculate the coordinates of the focus.

(d)   What is the equation of the directrix?

After working through this chapter you should:

1. be able to use algebra and geometry to fully justify and describe a conic given by a locus definition;

2. more specifically,

   (a) be able to recognise the various algebraic forms of each of the conics,

   (b) be able to construct the algebraic forms from the locus definition,

   (c) be aware of the symmetric properties of each conic,

   (d) be aware of special properties relating to each conic.

# *Parameters*

Curves can be represented by a set of equations, connected by a parameter. This form can sometimes have algebraic advantages over the Cartesian form and may also be easier to determine. The letter $t$ is often used for the parameter.

For a parabola two equations are required, one for $x$ in terms of $t$ and one for $y$ in terms of $t$.

Let $P$ have coordinates $(x, y)$ and make $x = t$, for an initial simple choice.

$$AP = PB \implies (a - t)^2 + y^2 = (t + a)^2$$
$$a^2 - 2at + t^2 + y^2 = t^2 + 2at + a^2$$
$$y^2 = 4at$$
$$y = 2\sqrt{(at)}$$

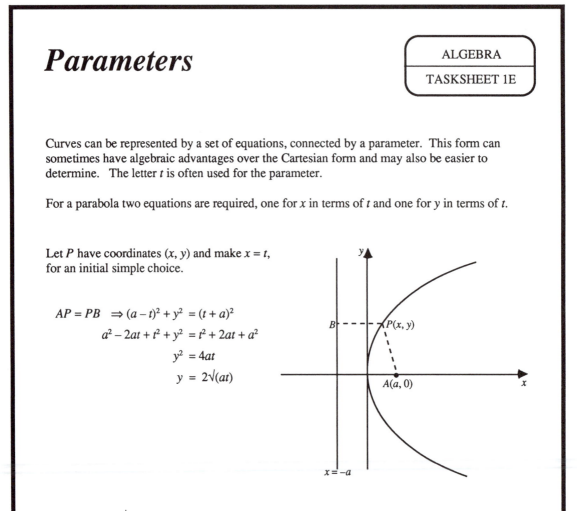

$x = t$ and $y = 2\sqrt{(at)}$ is a valid pair of equations but the square root can be an awkward function to handle. However, $2\sqrt{(at)}$ suggests that $y = 2at$ might be a good substitution. Then

$$(x + a)^2 = (a - x)^2 + 4a^2t^2$$
$$x^2 + 2ax + a^2 = a^2 - 2ax + x^2 + 4a^2t^2$$
$$4ax = 4a^2t^2$$
$$x = at^2$$

The form $x = at^2$, $y = 2at$ is, in fact, the usual parametric form of a parabola.

1    Obtain the Cartesian equation of the curve with parametric equations $x = 3t^2$ and $y = 6t$ by writing $t$ in terms of $y$ and substituting the expression for $t$ in $x = 3t^2$.

2    (a)    Obtain the Cartesian equation of the curve with parametric equations $x = 2at$ and $y = at^2$.

     (b)    Give a geometrical description of this curve.

# *a and b*

1    (a)   Show that the equation

$$\frac{x^2}{9} + \frac{y^2}{16} = 1$$

can be rearranged to give the two equations

$$y = 4\sqrt{\left(1 - \frac{x^2}{9}\right)} \text{ and } y = -4\sqrt{\left(1 - \frac{x^2}{9}\right)}$$

   (b)   Draw these two graphs on the same axes to given an ellipse.

   (c)   Where does the ellipse intersect the axes?

2    (a)   Draw the ellipse given by the equation

$$\frac{x^2}{25} + \frac{y^2}{4} = 1$$

   (b)   Where does this ellipse intersect the axes?

3    For the ellipse given by the equation

$$\frac{x^2}{a^2} + \frac{y^2}{b^2} = 1$$

where does this ellipse intersect the axes?  If necessary, draw some more examples.

4    (a)   Show that the equation

$$\frac{x^2}{9} - \frac{y^2}{16} = 1$$

can be rearranged to give the two equations

$$y = 4\sqrt{\left(\frac{x^2}{9} - 1\right)} \text{ and } y = -4\sqrt{\left(\frac{x^2}{9} - 1\right)}$$

   (b)   Draw these two graphs on the same axes to give an hyperbola.

   (c)   Where does the hyperbola intersect the *x*-axis?

   (d)   Draw on the same graph the lines $y = \frac{4}{3}x$ and $y = -\frac{4}{3}x$ .  How do these lines relate to the hyperbola?

5    For the hyperbola given by the equation

$$\frac{x^2}{a^2} - \frac{y^2}{b^2} = 1$$

   (a)   Where does the hyperbola intersect the *x*-axis?

   (b)   What will be given by the lines $y = \pm \frac{b}{a}x$ ?  (If necessary, draw some more examples.)

# *Facts and formulas*

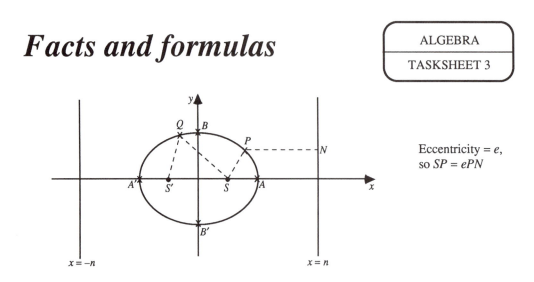

Eccentricity = $e$,
so $SP = ePN$

The general diagram given above allows a number of interesting facts to be derived for the ellipse. Note that $Q$ represents the pencil point in the pins and string locus construction and so $S'Q + SQ = l$, a constant distance.

Let the coordinates of the above points be as follows:

$$A(a, 0), A'(-a, 0), S(s, 0), S'(-s, 0), B(0, b) \text{ and } B'(0, -b)$$

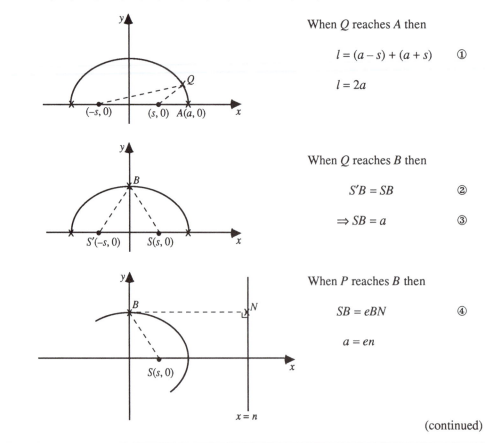

When $Q$ reaches $A$ then

$$l = (a - s) + (a + s) \qquad ①$$

$$l = 2a$$

When $Q$ reaches $B$ then

$$S'B = SB \qquad ②$$

$$\Rightarrow SB = a \qquad ③$$

When $P$ reaches $B$ then

$$SB = eBN \qquad ④$$

$$a = en$$

(continued)

50

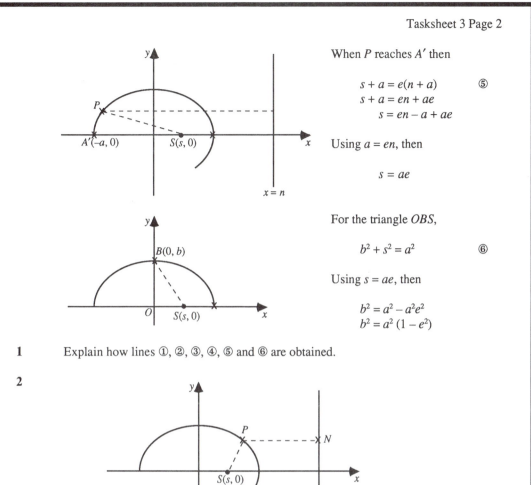

When $P$ reaches $A'$ then

$$s + a = e(n + a) \qquad \text{⑤}$$
$$s + a = en + ae$$
$$s = en - a + ae$$

Using $a = en$, then

$$s = ae$$

For the triangle $OBS$,

$$b^2 + s^2 = a^2 \qquad \text{⑥}$$

Using $s = ae$, then

$$b^2 = a^2 - a^2 e^2$$
$$b^2 = a^2 (1 - e^2)$$

**1**  Explain how lines ①, ②, ③, ④, ⑤ and ⑥ are obtained.

**2**

Let $P$ have coordinates $(x, y)$. Then, using $SP = ePN$,

$$\sqrt{((x - s)^2 + y^2)} = e(n - x) \qquad \text{⑦}$$

(a)  Show that ⑦ can be rearranged to give

$$x^2(1 - e^2) + 2x(ne^2 - s) + y^2 = e^2 n^2 - s^2 \qquad \text{⑧}$$

(b)  Using the facts obtained on this tasksheet, show that

   (i) $1 - e^2 = \dfrac{b^2}{a^2}$   (ii) $ne^2 - s = 0$   (iii) $e^2 n^2 - s^2 = b^2$

(c)  Hence show that ⑧ can be rearranged to

$$\frac{x^2}{a^2} + \frac{y^2}{b^2} = 1$$

the general equation of an ellipse, centre the origin.

# *Parametric form*

The parametric equations for a circle are

$$x = a \cos \theta$$

$$y = a \sin \theta$$

where $0° \leq \theta < 360°$

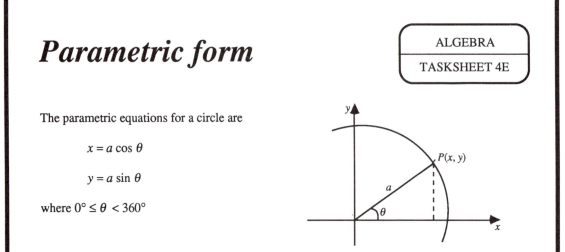

As previously stated a circle is a special case of an ellipse, where the major and minor axes are both the same.

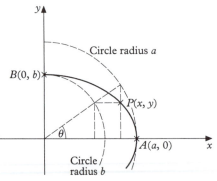

From the diagram the parametric form for the ellipse, based on the two circles, is

$$\left. \begin{array}{l} x = a \cos \theta \\ \\ y = b \sin \theta \end{array} \right\} \quad \text{where } 0° \leq \theta < 360°$$

All that is necessary to prove this is to show that

$$\frac{x^2}{a^2} + \frac{y^2}{b^2} = 1$$

**1**    Explain why this is 'all that is necessary'.

**2**    $\dfrac{x^2}{a^2} + \dfrac{y^2}{b^2} = \dfrac{a^2 \cos^2 \theta}{a^2} + \dfrac{b^2 \sin^2 \theta}{b^2}$

   $= \qquad\qquad ①$

   $= 1$

Fill in line ① and justify why this becomes 1, thus proving the validity of the parametric form.

# *Asymptotes*

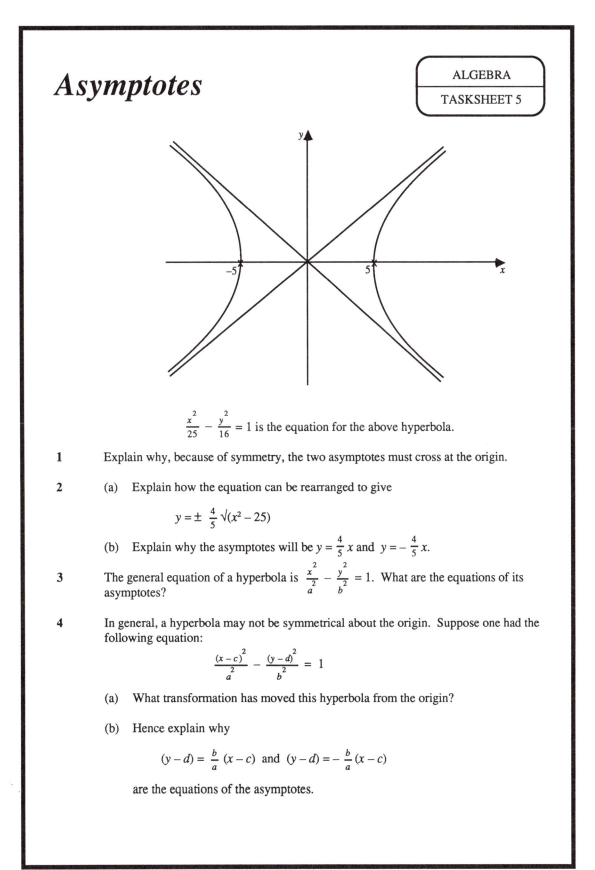

$\dfrac{x^2}{25} - \dfrac{y^2}{16} = 1$ is the equation for the above hyperbola.

1   Explain why, because of symmetry, the two asymptotes must cross at the origin.

2   (a)   Explain how the equation can be rearranged to give

$$y = \pm \, \tfrac{4}{5} \, \sqrt{(x^2 - 25)}$$

   (b)   Explain why the asymptotes will be $y = \dfrac{4}{5} x$ and $y = -\dfrac{4}{5} x$.

3   The general equation of a hyperbola is $\dfrac{x^2}{a^2} - \dfrac{y^2}{b^2} = 1$. What are the equations of its asymptotes?

4   In general, a hyperbola may not be symmetrical about the origin. Suppose one had the following equation:

$$\frac{(x - c)^2}{a^2} - \frac{(y - d)^2}{b^2} = 1$$

   (a)   What transformation has moved this hyperbola from the origin?

   (b)   Hence explain why

$$(y - d) = \frac{b}{a} \, (x - c) \ \text{ and } \ (y - d) = -\frac{b}{a} \, (x - c)$$

   are the equations of the asymptotes.

# *Tutorial sheet*

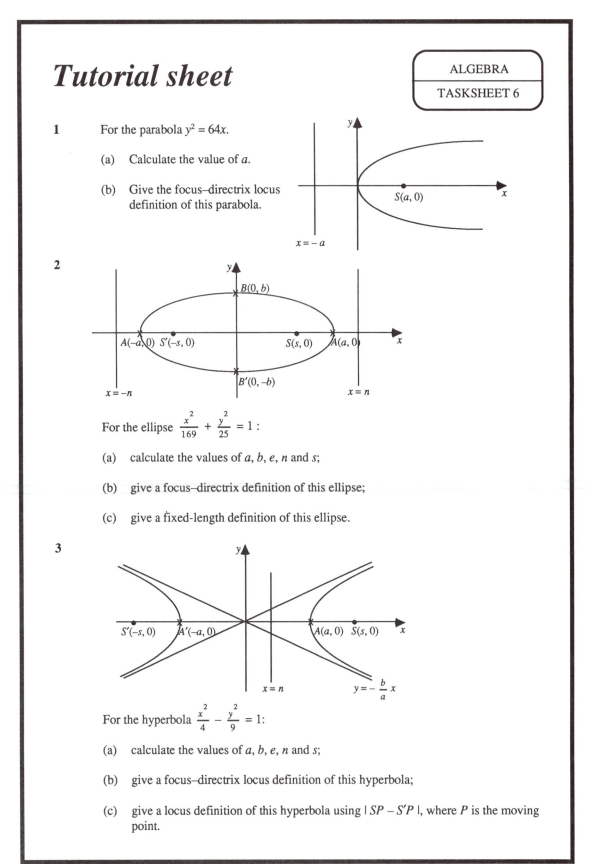

**1** For the parabola $y^2 = 64x$.

    (a)   Calculate the value of $a$.

    (b)   Give the focus–directrix locus definition of this parabola.

**2**

For the ellipse $\dfrac{x^2}{169} + \dfrac{y^2}{25} = 1$ :

    (a)   calculate the values of $a$, $b$, $e$, $n$ and $s$;

    (b)   give a focus–directrix definition of this ellipse;

    (c)   give a fixed-length definition of this ellipse.

**3**

For the hyperbola $\dfrac{x^2}{4} - \dfrac{y^2}{9} = 1$:

    (a)   calculate the values of $a$, $b$, $e$, $n$ and $s$;

    (b)   give a focus–directrix locus definition of this hyperbola;

    (c)   give a locus definition of this hyperbola using $|\,SP - S'P\,|$, where $P$ is the moving point.

# 5  *New worlds*

## 5.1  Definitions

There are infinitely many different loci. Mathematicians can consider various definitions and investigate which ones produce interesting outcomes. The previous four chapters have investigated and categorised some of the properties and principles of loci. This was done in the standard manner of starting with simple cases, and gradually and systematically increasing the complexity. En route, definitions were made, geometrical ideas were used to help recognise visual patterns and rigorous arguments were used to confirm these patterns.

This chapter looks at three alternative ways of creating new loci and in each case suggests possible lines for further investigation. If you pursue these, remember the following themes:

- be organised in your enquiries, considering simple cases first;

- search for potential patterns and properties;

- be systematic in looking at further cases;

- organise your findings, avoiding series of disjoint examples;

- formulate and generalise conjectures;

- use convincing arguments to justify your conjectures (these arguments will not always be algebraic);

- communicate your findings in an efficient and easy-to-read form.

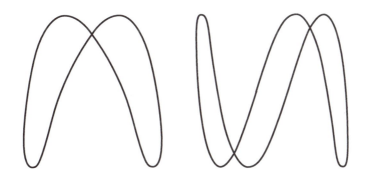

## 5.2    Basic constraints

The static constraint can be defined in many ways and, for more complex situations, moving components can be added to the definition. Many examples can be considered to be from the family of loci where there is an object along or around which a point is allowed to move.

### Example 1

Sketch the locus of the moving point $P$ with the following constraints.

Basic constraint

> $A$ is a fixed point, $BCD$ is a fixed triangle, $T$ is a point which is allowed to move around the triangle.

Dynamic constraint

> $P$ is the moving point such that $AP = \frac{1}{3} AT$.

### Solution

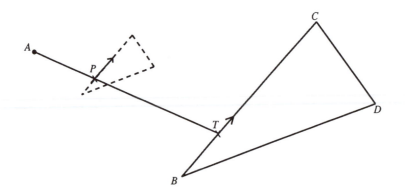

The locus of the moving point $P$ is a triangle which is an enlargement with centre $A$, scale factor $\frac{1}{3}$, of the triangle $BCD$.

TASKSHEET 1 – *Falling ladders (page 63)*

## 5.3 Nested loci

For nested loci the basic constraint is itself given by a locus definition.

Basic constraint

$A$ is a fixed point, $B$ is the moving point such that $AB = r_1$.

Dynamic constraint

$P$ is the moving point such that $BP = r_2$.

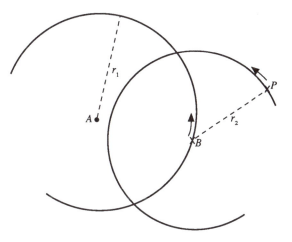

This gives a point moving around a circle, the centre of which is also a moving point on another circle.

TASKSHEET 2 – *The Octopus (page 64)*

The tasksheet has shown that the definition given above is in fact inadequate and the angular velocity of the moving point must also be stated. A correct general definition for an Octopus locus is therefore as follows.

Basic constraint

$A$ is a fixed point, $B$ is the moving point such that $AP = r_1$ and $B$ moves round $A$ with angular velocity $\omega_1$.

Dynamic constraint

$P$ is the moving point such that $BP = r_2$ and $P$ moves round $B$ with angular velocity $\omega_2$.

## 5.4    Metric spaces

When measuring or calculating distances on a grid the straight line definition based on Pythagoras is normally used. However, this is not always appropriate. For instance, in Milton Keynes the road system is based on a grid-like structure.

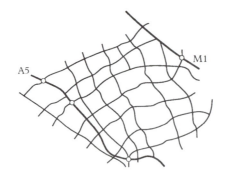

The organisation of the road system resembles a rectangular grid, with the roads labelled, for example, as H4 or V7, depending on whether they are 'horizontal' or 'vertical'.

In a road system, the distance between two places is not the straight line displacement but the sum of the 'horizontal' and 'vertical' displacements.

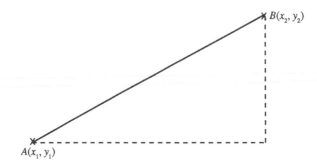

For the distance $AB$ above, this would be calculated in normal Euclidean geometry by

$$AB = \sqrt{((x_2 - x_1)^2 + (y_2 - y_1)^2)}$$

But in **Taxicab geometry**, a title based on the analogy with road systems, the distance $AB$ is calculated using horizontal and vertical displacements by

$$AB = |x_2 - x_1| + |y_2 - y_1|$$

This 'distance' can be denoted by $d_t(A, B)$.

Such a change in calculating distances produces what is called a **metric space** in which all the rules of geometry and algebra must be checked. Investigating what happens to loci in a new metric space can produce some unexpected results. Some properties stay the same whereas others are totally different.

## Example 2

Using Taxicab geometry, sketch the locus of the moving point $P$ such that $AP = 5$, where $A$ is a fixed point.

## Solution

On squared paper, label the distance of each point from $A$. Then join all the points together.

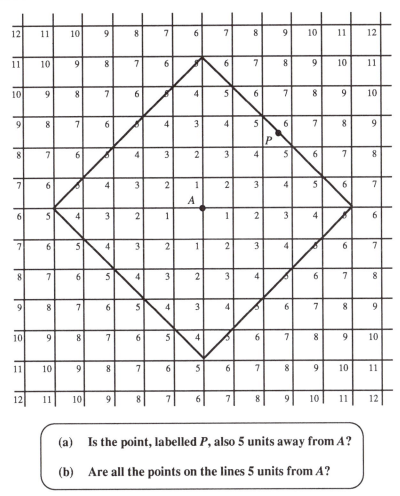

> (a)  Is the point, labelled $P$, also 5 units away from $A$?
>
> (b)  Are all the points on the lines 5 units from $A$?

This technique is simple and easy to use. Although it is slow, it prevents the making of errors caused by jumping too rapidly to conclusions about the properties of a new metric space.

The locus of $P$ is called a **Taxicab circle** because it has the same definition as a Euclidean circle. However, it does look a little different!

   TASKSHEET 3 – *Apollonius' circles (page 65)*

## 5.5    Further investigations

For at least one of these investigations, it is expected that you will

*   investigate a simple case;

*   vary constraints in a structured manner so that many cases may be categorised;

*   formulate general conjectures;

*   give convincing reasons for these conjectures.


### A    Sliding ladders

Investigate the locus of the moving point $P$ such that $AP = \lambda BP$ where $A$ moves along a line $l$, $B$ moves along a line $m$ and $AB = k$, a fixed length.

### B    Petals

$Q$ is a point on the edge of a circle radius $r_Q$, rotating at a given angular velocity $\omega_Q$ about the centre $A$, a fixed point. Investigate the locus of the moving point $P$, where $P$ is on the edge of a circle, radius $r_p$, rotating at a given angular velocity $\omega_p$ about the centre, $Q$.

### C    Apollonius' Taxicab circles

Using Taxicab geometry, investigate the locus of the moving point $P$ such that for two distinct points $A$ and $B$, $d_t(A, P) = \lambda d_t(B, P)$.

### D    Taxicab ellipses

Using Taxicab geometry, investigate the locus of the moving point $P$ such that for two distinct points $A$ and $B$, $d_t(A, P) + d_t(B, P) = k$.

### E    Taxicab hyperbola

Using Taxicab geometry, investigate the locus of the moving point $P$ such that for two distinct points $A$ and $B$, $|d_t(A, P) - d_t(B, P)| = k$.

### F    Taxicab parabolas

Using Taxicab geometry, investigate the locus of the moving point $P$ such that for a distinct point $S$ and fixed line $l$, $d_t(P, S) = d_t(P, l)$.

## G    Taxicab circular functions

For a circle in Euclidean geometry, the ratio of $\frac{y}{r}$ for all values of $\theta$ defines the circular function sin $\theta$.

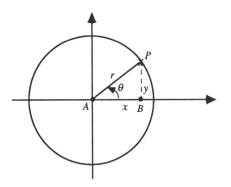

Using a Taxicab circle, investigate the Taxicab sine function, that is

$$\sin{}_t \theta = \frac{d_t(B, P)}{d_t(A, P)}$$

## H    Toppling polygons

Investigate the locus of the moving point $P$, where $P$ is a vertex of a polygon which is rolling along a horizontal surface.

## I    Your own investigations

Any locus situation investigated should give the opportunity to demonstrate the processes given at the start of this chapter.

## HINTS:

**A:**    Start with $l$ and $m$ at right angles, then consider other angles.

**B:**    Consider the effect of different radii for the circles and the effect of changing the directions of rotation.

**C:**    Taking $A$ and $B$ on a horizontal line, consider $0 < \lambda < 1$, $\lambda > 1$ and $\lambda = 1$. Then allow $B$ to move around $A$, giving $AB$ as a sloping line.

**D:**    Take $AB$ horizontal, vertical and then sloping.

**E:**    Take $AB$ horizontal, vertical and then sloping.

**F:**    Start with $l$ vertical and then rotate it.

**G:**    Look at solving equations and other circular function ideas.

**H:**    Perhaps consider regular polygons beginning with triangles, or consider a polygon with a fixed number of sides of varying lengths.

After working through this chapter you should be able to:

1    appreciate the potentially infinite variety of loci;

2    structure an investigation and

    (a)    recognise patterns and properties;

    (b)    generalise these ideas;

    (c)    produce convincing arguments to support
           your findings.

# *Falling ladders*

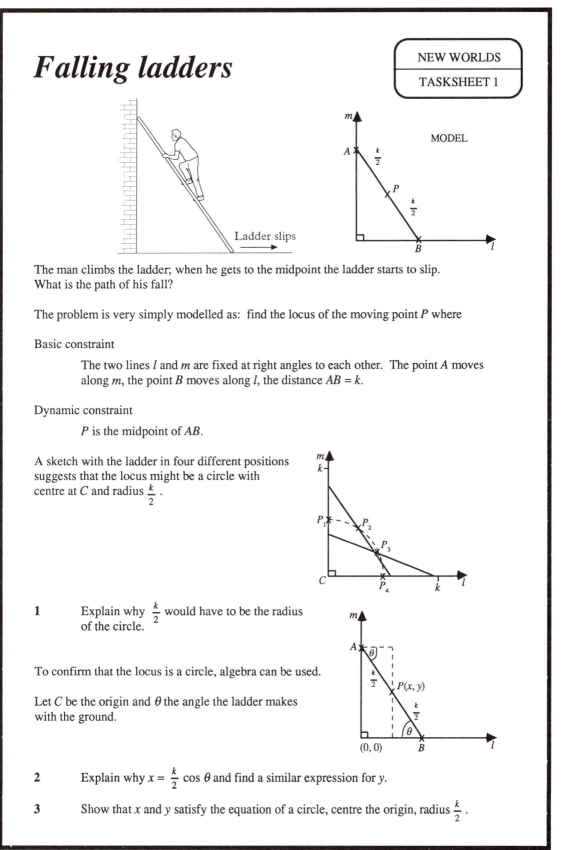

MODEL

The man climbs the ladder; when he gets to the midpoint the ladder starts to slip. What is the path of his fall?

The problem is very simply modelled as: find the locus of the moving point $P$ where

Basic constraint

> The two lines $l$ and $m$ are fixed at right angles to each other. The point $A$ moves along $m$, the point $B$ moves along $l$, the distance $AB = k$.

Dynamic constraint

> $P$ is the midpoint of $AB$.

A sketch with the ladder in four different positions suggests that the locus might be a circle with centre at $C$ and radius $\frac{k}{2}$ .

**1**    Explain why $\frac{k}{2}$ would have to be the radius of the circle.

To confirm that the locus is a circle, algebra can be used.

Let $C$ be the origin and $\theta$ the angle the ladder makes with the ground.

**2**    Explain why $x = \frac{k}{2} \cos \theta$ and find a similar expression for $y$.

**3**    Show that $x$ and $y$ satisfy the equation of a circle, centre the origin, radius $\frac{k}{2}$ .

# *The Octopus*

The *Octopus* is a commonly
seen fairground ride in which
the chairs rotate about the end
of large rotating arms. In one
version of this ride, the chair
reaches the outside edge
moving slowly, turns, moves
rapidly under the large rotating
arm and reaches the outside
edge, again moving slowly.

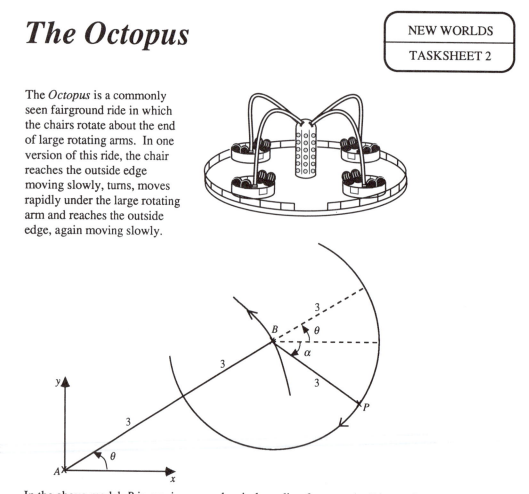

In the above model, *B* is moving around a circle, radius 6, centre *A*. *P* is moving around a circle,
radius 3, centre *B*. *B* is moving anti-clockwise and *P* is moving clockwise around the circles.
The coordinates of *P* are given by

$$x = 6 \cos \theta + 3 \cos \alpha$$

$$y = 6 \sin \theta - 3 \sin \alpha$$

Using a parametric graph plotter, obtain the locus of the moving point *P* when:

1      $\theta = t$ and $\alpha = \dfrac{7t}{3}$

2      $\theta = t$ and $\alpha = 2t$

3      $\theta = t$ and $\alpha = 7t$

4      $\theta = t$ and $\alpha = \dfrac{t}{2}$

[Note: Measuring $\theta$ and $\alpha$ in degrees, using a range of 0 to 360 for *t* may not be sufficient to
sketch the whole locus.]

# *Apollonius' circles*

NEW WORLDS

TASKSHEET 3

The locus definition for Apollonius' circles was investigated in Chapter 2. This can also be considered in Taxicab geometry.

Static constraint

Let $A$ and $B$ be two fixed points.

Dynamic constraint

$P$ is the moving point such that $AP = 3BP$.

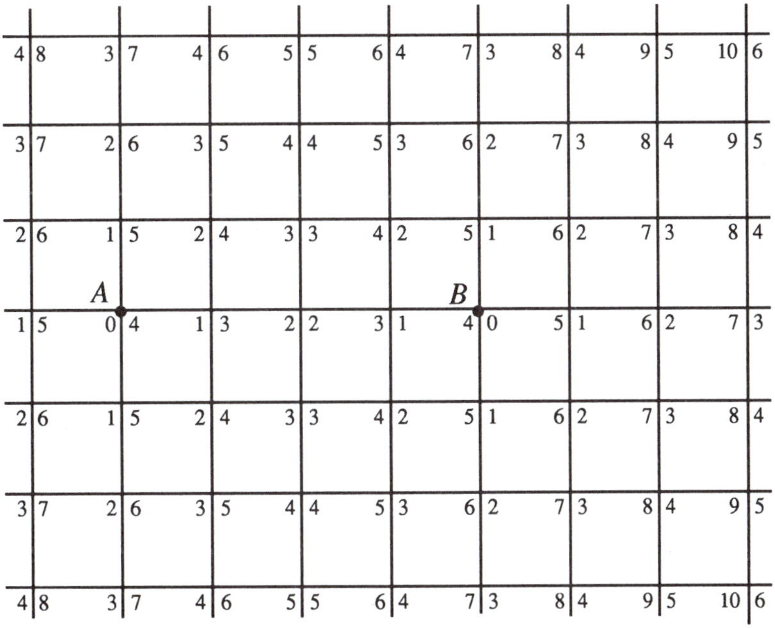

4 8 3 7 4 6 5 5 6 4 7 3 8 4 9 5 10 6
3 7 2 6 3 5 4 4 5 3 6 2 7 3 8 4 9 5
2 6 1 5 2 4 3 3 4 2 5 1 6 2 7 3 8 4
A
B
1 5 0 4 1 3 2 2 3 1 4 0 5 1 6 2 7 3
2 6 1 5 2 4 3 3 4 2 5 1 6 2 7 3 8 4
3 7 2 6 3 5 4 4 5 3 6 2 7 3 8 4 9 5
4 8 3 7 4 6 5 5 6 4 7 3 8 4 9 5 10 6


Squared paper can be labelled with distances from $A$ on the left and distances from $B$ on the right.

**1** Copy the above diagram and draw in the locus of $P$.

**2** Is the resulting shape a Taxicab circle?

# SOLUTIONS

# 1 Circles

## 1.1 Fixed points, moving points

> **(a)** What is the length of $h$?
>
> **(b)** What is the path of $P$? (N.B. the path of $P$ is in two parts.)

(a) $\frac{1}{2} \times 10 \times h = 30$, so $h = 6$ cm.

(b) The path of $P$ consists of two lines, one above and one below $AB$, both parallel to $AB$ and 6 cm away from it.

## 1.2 The locus of a circle

> Explain why, for any $(x, y)$,
>
> $x^2 + y^2 = 300^2$.

For any $(x, y)$ a right-angled triangle is obtained, with hypotenuse of length 300 and the other two sides of lengths $x$ and $y$.

So Pythagoras' Theorem gives $x^2 + y^2 = 300^2$.

## 1.3 Moving from the origin

> Explain why the equation
>
> $x^2 - 10x + 4xy + y^2 - 8y - 4 = 0$
>
> cannot be the equation of a circle.

The equation of a circle cannot contain a term in $xy$.

**Exercise 1**

1  (a)  $x^2 + (y-4)^2 = 5^2 = 25$

   (b)  $(x+3)^2 + (y-2)^2 = 3^2 = 9$

2  (a)  Centre (2, 0) and radius 8.  $(x-2)^2 + y^2 = 64$

   (b)  Centre (8, 5) and radius $\sqrt{13}$.  $(x-8)^2 + (y-5)^2 = 13$

3  $r = \sqrt{(5^2 + 12^2)} = 13$.  $(x-2)^2 + (y-5)^2 = 169$

4  (a)  Equation rearranges to $(x-2)^2 + (y-3)^2 = 9$,
        so gives a circle centre (2, 3) and radius 3.

   (b)  The equation contains an $xy$ term, so does not give a circle.

   (c)  Equation rearranges to $(x-4)^2 + y^2 = 16$,
        so gives a circle centre (4, 0) and radius 4.

   (d)  Equation rearranges to $(x+2)^2 + (y-2)^2 = 16$,
        so gives a circle centre (–2, 2) and radius 4.

   (e)  There is no term in $y^2$, so the equation does not give a circle.

   (f)  Equation rearranges to $(x+6)^2 + (y-2)^2 = 64$,
        so gives a circle centre (–6, 2) and radius 8.

# 2 Constraints

## 2.1 Perpendicular bisector

> **What is the equation of the locus of a point equidistant from $A(3, -1)$ and $B(3, 5)$?**

The equation of the locus is $y = 2$.

## 2.2 For any ratio

> **Explain why:**
>
> (a) $OP = \sqrt{(x^2 + y^2)}$
>
> (b) $AP = \sqrt{((3 - x)^2 + y^2)}$

$OT = x$ and $PT = y$, so $OP = \sqrt{(x^2 + y^2)}$

$AT = 3 - x$ and $PT = y$, so $AP = \sqrt{((3 - x)^2 + y^2)}$

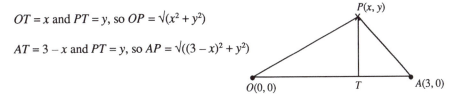

### Exercise 1

**1** (a)

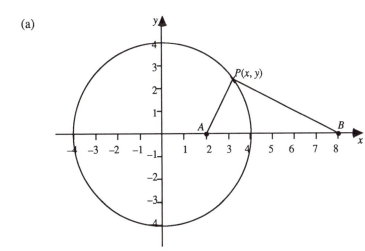

(b) $\sqrt{((8-x)^2 + y^2)} = 2\sqrt{((x-2)^2 + y^2)}$

$(8-x)^2 + y^2 = 4((x-2)^2 + y^2)$

$64 - 16x + x^2 + y^2 = 4(x^2 - 4x + 4 + y^2)$

$64 - 16x + x^2 + y^2 = 4x^2 - 16x + 16 + 4y^2$

$3x^2 + 3y^2 = 48$

$x^2 + y^2 = 16$

(c) The equation is that of a circle with centre $(0, 0)$ and radius 4.

**2** (a) $\sqrt{(x^2 + y^2)} = 3\sqrt{((4-x)^2 + y^2)}$

$x^2 + y^2 = 9((4-x)^2 + y^2)$

$x^2 + y^2 = 9(16 - 8x + x^2 + y^2)$

$x^2 + y^2 = 144 - 72x + 9x^2 + 9y^2$

$8x^2 + 8y^2 - 72x + 144 = 0$

$x^2 + y^2 - 9x + 18 = 0$

(b) Equation rearranges to $(x - 4.5)^2 + y^2 = 2.25$.

The locus is a circle with centre $(4.5, 0)$ and radius 1.5.

**3E** $\sqrt{(x^2 + y^2)} = 2\sqrt{((a-x)^2 + y^2)}$

$x^2 + y^2 = 4((a-x)^2 + y^2)$

$x^2 + y^2 = 4(a^2 - 2ax + x^2 + y^2)$

$x^2 + y^2 = 4a^2 - 8ax + 4x^2 + 4y^2$

$3x^2 + 3y^2 - 8ax + 4a^2 = 0$

$x^2 + y^2 - \frac{8}{3}ax + \frac{4}{3}a^2 = 0$

$(x - \frac{4}{3}a)^2 + y^2 = -\frac{4}{3}a^2 + \frac{16}{9}a^2$

$(x - \frac{4}{3}a)^2 + y^2 = \frac{4}{9}a^2$

The locus is a circle with centre $(\frac{4}{3}a, 0)$ and radius $\frac{2}{3}a$.

**4E** (a) $\sqrt{(x^2 + y^2)} = \lambda\sqrt{((a-x)^2 + y^2)}$

$x^2 + y^2 = \lambda^2((a-x)^2 + y^2)$

$x^2 + y^2 = \lambda^2(a^2 - 2ax + x^2 + y^2)$

$x^2 + y^2 = \lambda^2 a^2 - 2\lambda^2 ax + \lambda^2 x^2 + \lambda^2 y^2$

$x^2(\lambda^2 - 1) + y^2(\lambda^2 - 1) - 2a\lambda^2 x + \lambda^2 a^2 = 0$

$x^2 + y^2 - \frac{2a\lambda^2}{\lambda^2 - 1}x + \frac{\lambda^2 a^2}{\lambda^2 - 1} = 0$

$\left(x - \frac{a\lambda^2}{\lambda^2 - 1}\right)^2 + y^2 = \frac{a^2\lambda^4}{(\lambda^2 - 1)^2} - \frac{\lambda^2 a^2}{\lambda^2 - 1}$

$= \frac{a^2\lambda^2}{(\lambda^2 - 1)^2}$

(b)  The circle has centre $\left( \dfrac{a\lambda^2}{\lambda^2 - 1}, 0 \right)$ and radius $\dfrac{a\lambda}{\lambda^2 - 1}$.

(c)  When $a = 0$, radius $= 0$.  Since $O$ and $A$ now coincide, there is no circle.

(d)  When $\lambda = 1$, radius is undefined.  Since $PO = PA$, the locus is the perpendicular bisector of $OA$ (a straight line).

## 2.3  More equations

**Exercise 2**

1  (a)

$$P_2 \qquad\qquad A \quad P_1 \qquad\qquad B$$
$$(p_2, 0) \qquad\quad (2, 0)\ (p_1, 0) \qquad (8, 0)$$

$$8 - p_1 = 2(p_1 - 2) \qquad\qquad 8 - p_2 = 2(2 - p_2)$$
$$8 - p_1 = 2p_1 - 4 \qquad\qquad 8 - p_2 = 4 - 2p_2$$
$$p_1 = 4 \qquad\qquad\qquad\quad p_2 = -4$$

The points are $(4, 0)$ and $(-4, 0)$.

(b)  The locus is a circle centre $(0, 0)$ and radius 4, so its equation is $x^2 + y^2 = 16$.

2  The two points on the locus which are on the line joining $A$ and $B$ have coordinates $(0, 0)$ and $(-6, 0)$.  The locus is a circle with centre $(-3, 0)$ and radius 3.  Its equation is $(x + 3)^2 + y^2 = 9$.

3  The two points on the locus which are on the line joining $A$ and $B$ have coordinates $(8, 0)$ and $(16, 0)$.  The locus is a circle with centre $(12, 0)$ and radius 4.  Its equation is $(x - 12)^2 + y^2 = 16$.

4  The two points on the lcous which are on the line joining $A$ and $B$ have coordinates $(6, 0)$ and $(-2, 0)$.  The locus is a circle with centre $(2, 0)$ and radius 4. Its equation is $(x - 2)^2 + y^2 = 16$.

5E  (a)  Let $C$ be the point $(x_1, y_1)$

Then $\quad 34 - x_1 = 3(x_1 - 2) \Rightarrow x_1 = 10$
$\qquad\quad 26 - y_1 = 3(y_1 - 2) \Rightarrow y_1 = 8$

$C$ is the point $(10, 8)$

Let $D$ be the point $(x_2, y_2)$

Then $\quad 34 - x_2 = 3(2 - x_2) \Rightarrow x_2 = -14$
$\qquad\quad 26 - y_2 = 3(2 - y_2) \Rightarrow y_2 = -10$

$D$ is the point $(-14, -10)$

(b)  The locus is a circle with centre $(-2, -1)$ and radius 15.  Its equation is $(x + 2)^2 + (y + 1)^2 = 225$.

## 2.4 Fixing an angle

> **Using an argument based upon symmetry, justify why $x = 90$ gives a circle.**

If $x < 90$, two major arcs are obtained.

If $x > 90$, two minor arcs are obtained.

$x = 90$ gives two semicircles, so the complete locus is a circle.

## 2.5 Proved and used

**Exercise 3**

**1**

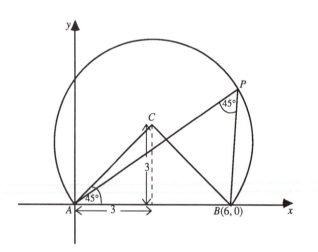

(a)   $ACB = 90°$

(b)   $C$ is the point $(3, 3)$.

(c)   $r = \sqrt{(3^2 + 3^2)} = 4.24$ (to 2 decimal places)

(d)   The locus is a major arc of the circle

$$(x - 3)^2 + (y - 3)^2 = 18$$

**2**     Let $C$ be the centre of the circle, so $A\hat{C}B = 140°$. Let $D$ be the midpoint of $AB$.

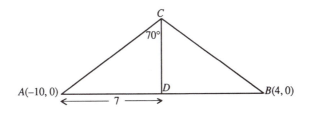

$CD = \dfrac{7}{\tan 70°} = 2.55$ (to 2 decimal places)

The centre of the circle has coordinates $(-3, 2.55)$ and radius $\dfrac{7}{\sin 70°} = 7.45$ (to 2 decimal places).

The locus is a major arc of the circle $(x + 3)^2 + (y - 2.55)^2 = 55.5$. This is the equation of the part of the locus above $AB$. The locus for the situation when $P$ is below $AB$ will be part of a circle with centre $(-3, -2.55)$, radius 7.45 and equation $(x + 3)^2 + (y + 2.55)^2 = 55.5$.

**3**     Since the angle subtended is 90° the locus is a circle. The circle has centre $(8, 0)$, radius 4 and equation $(x - 8)^2 + y^2 = 16$.

**4E**   (a)   $ACB = 60°$

(b)   Since $AC = CB$ and $ACB = 60°$, the triangle $ABC$ is equilaterial, with each side of length 4. The height of the triangle $ABC = \sqrt{(4^2 - 2^2)} = \sqrt{12}$. So $C$ is the point $(2, -\sqrt{12})$.

(c)   Radius $= 4$

(d)   The locus is a minor arc of the circle $(x - 2)^2 + (y + \sqrt{12})^2 = 16$.

# 3   Conics

## 3.1   Cutting a cone

> **What is the cross-section of a cone?**

A circle.

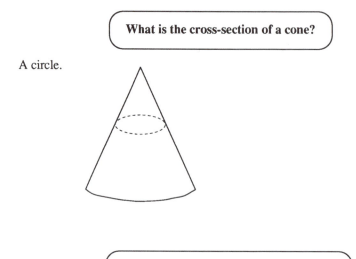

> **Describe some other situations in which these curves are involved.**

Parabolic mirrors are used in telescopes and car headlights.

Hyperbolas are found in graphs connected with Boyle's law.

Cooling towers at power stations are the shape formed by rotating a hyperbola about a vertical axis.

## 3.2   Focus and directrix

> **Why is *BP* at a right angle to the directrix?**

The shortest distance from a point to a line is the one measured at right angles to the line.

**Exercise 1**

1   (a)   The locus is an ellipse.

    (b)   The two points are (2, 0) and (–6, 0).

(c)

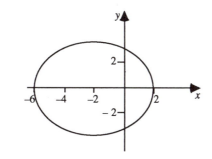

**2** (a) The locus is a hyperbola.

(b) The 2 points are (4, 0) and (12, 0).

(c)

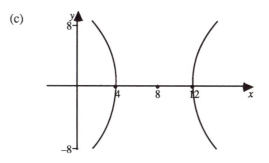

**3** The two definitions give the same locus since

$$PN' = P'N$$
$$PS' = P'S$$

$$P'N = 2\,P'S \text{ and so}$$

$$PN' = 2\,PS'$$

**4** (a)  (b)

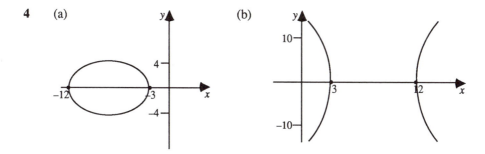

(c)

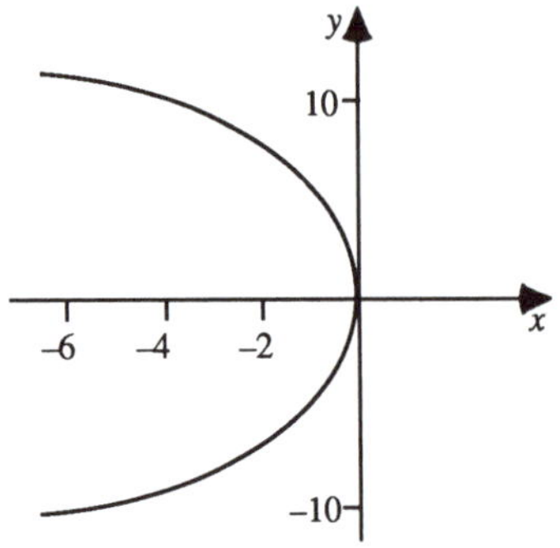


(d)

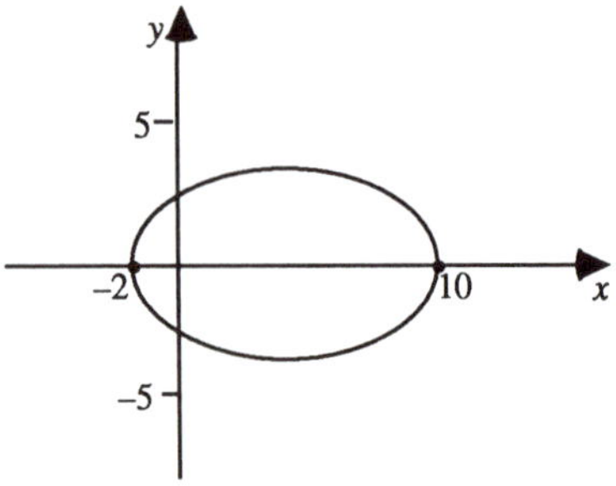


(e)

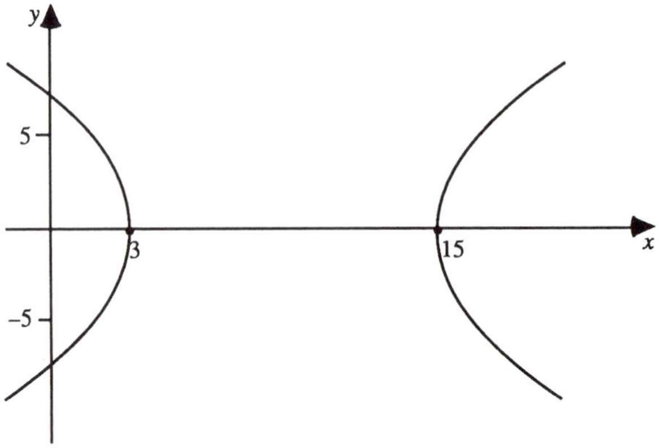


**5** (a) The ellipses, (a) and (d), and the hyperbolas, (b) and (e).

(b) For (a), focus (–9, 0) directrix $x = -21$.

For (b), focus (21, 0), directrix $x = 9$.

For (d), focus (8, 0) directrix $x = 13$.

For (e), focus (18, 0), directrix $x = 13$.

## 3.3 Pins and strings

> **(a) What conic section does this produce?**
>
> **(b) Give a locus definition based on this idea.**

(a) This produces an ellipse. The pins are the positions of the two foci of the ellipse.

(b) The point $P$ moves such that, for two distinct points $A$ and $B$, $AP + PB = \lambda$, where $\lambda$ is a fixed value.

# 4 Algebra

## 4.1 Parabolas

> **(a)** Explain line ①.
>
> **(b)** 'Because $a$ is in the equation the parabola obtained is dependent on the value of $a$.'
>
> What does this statement mean?

(a) $x + a$ is the shortest distance from $p$ to the line $x = -a$.

By Pythagoras, $\sqrt{((a-x)^2 + y^2)}$ is the distance from $P$ to the focus. For a parabola, these two distances must be equal.

(b) The statement means that changing the value of $a$ will change the equation of the parabola.

### Exercise 1

1    (a)   $y^2 = 200(x - 50) \Rightarrow y = \pm\sqrt{(200(x - 50))}$, so the curve is symmetrical about the $x$-axis.

      (b)   When $y = 0$, $200(x - 50) = 0$, so $x = 50$. The curve crosses the $x$-axis at $(50, 0)$.

      (c)   $y^2 = 200x$ would be a parabola with focus at $(50, 0)$ and directrix $x = -50$.

          $y^2 = 200(x - 50)$ is a transation of this parabola by the vector $\begin{bmatrix} 50 \\ 0 \end{bmatrix}$ so has focus $(100, 0)$ and directrix $x = 0$.

2    Let $P$ be the point $(x, y)$.

$$PS = \sqrt{(x^2 + y^2)} \qquad PN = 4 - x$$

So   $x^2 + y^2 = (4 - x)^2$

      $x^2 + y^2 = 16 - 8x + x^2$

          $y^2 = 16 - 8x$

**3**

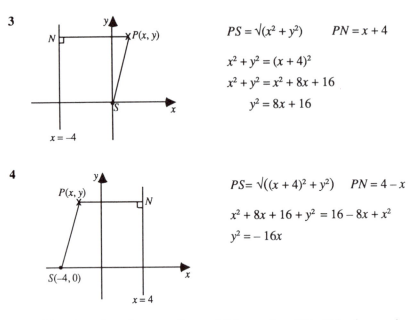

$$PS = \sqrt{(x^2 + y^2)} \qquad PN = x + 4$$

$$x^2 + y^2 = (x + 4)^2$$
$$x^2 + y^2 = x^2 + 8x + 16$$
$$y^2 = 8x + 16$$

**4**

$$PS = \sqrt{((x + 4)^2 + y^2)} \qquad PN = 4 - x$$

$$x^2 + 8x + 16 + y^2 = 16 - 8x + x^2$$
$$y^2 = -16x$$

(Note that, since the $x$-coordinate of $P$ is negative, $PN$ will be $4 - x$ and not $4 + x$.)

**5**  $\quad PN = y + a \qquad\qquad PS = \sqrt{(x^2 + (a - y)^2)}$

$$(y + a)^2 = x^2 + (a - y)^2$$
$$y^2 + 2ay + a^2 = x^2 + a^2 - 2ay + y^2$$
$$x^2 = 4ay$$

## 4.2   Equations

> **Why has the answer to (b) been left in surd form?**

The answer has been left in surd form because the **exact** value of $b$ was asked for. Also, since the equation requires $b^2$, there is no point in evaluating the square root to obtain a numerical approximation for $b$.

**Exercise 2**

**1**   (a)   $a - s$ is the distance from $A$ to $S$ and $n - a$ is the distance from $A$ to the line $x = n$. As the curve is an ellipse:

$$a - s = e(n - a), \text{ and so } a - s = en - ea \quad ①$$

The distance from $A'$ to $S$ is $a + s$ and the distance from $A'$ to the line $x = n$ is $n + a$. So

$$a + s = e(n + a) = en + ea \quad ②$$

(b) Subtracting the equations in (a) from each other gives

$$2s = 2ea, \text{ so } ae = s$$

(c) $5 = 0.25a$, so $a = 20$

The use of either of the equations in (a) gives $n = 80$.

(d) Let $B$ be the point $(0, b)$.

$$BS = \sqrt{(b^2 + s^2)} = \sqrt{(b^2 + 25)}$$

The distance from $B$ to $x = n$ is $n$.

$$\sqrt{(b^2 + 25)} = 0.25n = 20$$

$$b^2 + 25 = 400, \text{ so } b = \sqrt{375}$$

The equation of the ellipse is $\dfrac{x^2}{400} + \dfrac{y^2}{375} = 1$.

**2** (a)

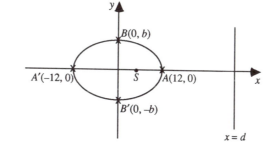

(b) $12 - s = \dfrac{1}{3}(d - 12) = \dfrac{1}{3}d - 4$ (using $A$)

$12 + s = \dfrac{1}{3}(d + 12) = \dfrac{1}{3}d + 4$ (using $A'$)

Adding the equations gives

$$24 = \dfrac{2}{3}d, \text{ so } d = 36$$

Subtracting the equations gives

$$2s = 8, \text{ so } s = 4$$

(c) $\sqrt{(b^2 + 16)} = \dfrac{1}{3}d$

$b^2 + 16 = \dfrac{1}{9}d^2 = 144 \text{ so } b = \sqrt{128}$

(d) $\dfrac{x^2}{144} + \dfrac{y^2}{128} = 1$

**3**    (a)    $a = 5$ and $\dfrac{b}{a} = \dfrac{1}{2}$, so $b = 2.5$

The equation is $\dfrac{x^2}{25} - \dfrac{y^2}{6.25} = 1$.

(b)

$\tan \theta = \dfrac{1}{2}$ , so $\theta = 26.6°$ (to 1 decimal place)

## 4.3    Ellipses

> Why could the definition of this ellipse also be based on $S'$, $x = -n$ and $e$?

From the symmetry of the situation, $AS = A'S'$ and the distance from $A$ to $x = n$ is the same as the distance from $A'$ to $x = -n$.

> (a)    Explain how the ellipse varies as $a$ and $e$ are varied.
>
> (b)    What is obtained for the extreme values of $e$, which are 0 and 1?

(a)    As $a$ increases, the ellipse is enlarged.

For small values of $e$, the height of the ellipse is close to its length and as $e$ increases the ratio of height to length decreases.

(b)    When $e = 0$, $b^2 = a^2$, so a circle is obtained, the focus is the origin and the directrix is undefined. $SP \neq 0$ but as $e \to 0$, $SP \to a$.

When $e = 1$, $b^2 = 0$, giving a line along the $x$-axis, the focus and directrix are co-incident.

**Exercise 3**

**1**    (a)

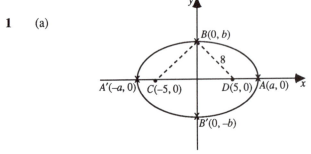

(b)  If point $A$ is on the locus, $(a - 5) + (a + 5) = 16$, so $a = 8$.
The major axis is of length 16.
If point $B$ is on the locus, $b^2 = 64 - 25 = 39$
The minor axis is of length $2\sqrt{39}$.

(c)  Using $b^2 = a^2 (1 - e^2)$:

$$39 = 64(1 - e^2)$$

$$1 - e^2 = \frac{39}{64} \text{ , so } e^2 = \frac{25}{64} \text{ and } e = \frac{5}{8}$$

(d)  $n = \dfrac{a}{e} = \dfrac{8}{5/8} = \dfrac{64}{5} = 12.8$

The equations of the two possible directrices are $x = 12.8$ and $x = -12.8$.

(e)  The equation is $\dfrac{x^2}{64} + \dfrac{y^2}{39} = 1$.

**2**  $a = \dfrac{s}{e} = \dfrac{3}{3/5} = 5$

$n = \dfrac{a}{e} = \dfrac{5}{3/5} = \dfrac{25}{3}$, so the equation of the directrix is $x = \dfrac{25}{3}$.

$b^2 = a^2(1 - e^2) = 25 \left(1 - \dfrac{9}{25}\right) = 25 \times \dfrac{16}{25}$

$b^2 = 16$, so the coordinates of $B$ are $(0, 4)$ and of $B'$ are $(0, -4)$.

The equation of the ellipse is $\dfrac{x^2}{25} + \dfrac{y^2}{16} = 1$.

**3**  (a)  $a - s = e(n - a) = en - ea$

$a + s = e(n + a) = en + ea$

$2a = 2en \Rightarrow a = en$  ①

$2s = 2ea \Rightarrow s = ae$  ②

(b)  $\sqrt{(b^2 + s^2)} = en$

$b^2 + s^2 = e^2n^2$

$b^2 = e^2n^2 - s^2$

(c)  From ① and ②  $en = a$  (so $e^2n^2 = a^2$)

and  $s = ae$

$b^2 = a^2 - a^2e^2$

$b^2 = a^2 (1 - e^2)$

## 4.4 Hyperbolas

> **Explain how the hyperbola varies as $a$ and $e$ are varied.**

As $a$ increases the branches of the hyperbola cut the $x$-axis further from the origin and the branches of the hyperbola become less steep.

As $e$ increases the branches of the hyperbola become steeper.

### Exercise 4

**1**　(a)　$(a, 0)$ is on the locus so: $12 - a = e(a - 3)$
$(-a, 0)$ is on the locus so: $12 + a = e(a + 3)$

$$24 = 2ae \Rightarrow ae = 12 \quad \text{①}$$
$$2a = 6e \Rightarrow a = 3e \quad \text{②}$$

From ① and ②　$3e^2 = 12$
$$e = 2$$
Hence　$a = 6$

OR　　Quoting　$s = ae$ with $s = 12$ gives $12 = ae$
$a = en$ with $n = 3$ gives $a = 3e$
$3e^2 = 12$, as before.

(b)　$a^2 = 36$　　$b^2 = 36(e^2 - 1) = 36(4 - 1) = 108$

The equation is $\dfrac{x^2}{36} - \dfrac{y^2}{108} = 1$.

**2**　(a)　If the focus is $(s, 0)$ and directrix $x = n$, then:

$$s = ae \text{ and } a = en$$

but $e = 4$ and $n = \dfrac{1}{2}$ so　$a = 2$
$$s = 4 \times 2 = 8$$

The focus is at $(8, 0)$.

(b)　$a^2 = 4$　　$b^2 = a^2(e^2 - 1) = 60$

The equation is $\dfrac{x^2}{4} - \dfrac{y^2}{60} = 1$.

**3**　The asymptotes have gradients $\pm \dfrac{b}{a}$ .

$$b^2 = a^2 (e^2 - 1) \text{ and } e = \sqrt{2}$$
$$b^2 = a^2(2 - 1)$$
$$b^2 = a^2$$
$$\frac{b^2}{a^2} = 1$$

So the asymptotes have gradients $\pm 1$.

**4** (a)  When $y = 0$, $x^2 = 25$.

The hyperbola cuts the $x$-axis at $(5, 0)$ and $(-5, 0)$.

(b)  $a^2 = 25$     $b^2 = 39$

so $39 = 25\,(e^2 - 1)$

$e^2 - 1 = \dfrac{39}{25}$

$e^2 = \dfrac{39}{25} + 1 = \dfrac{64}{25}$

$e = \dfrac{8}{5}$

(c)  $s = ae = 5 \times \dfrac{8}{5}$

The focus is at $(8, 0)$.

(d)  $a = en$ so $n = \dfrac{a}{e} = \dfrac{5}{8/5} = \dfrac{25}{8}$

The directrix is $x = \dfrac{25}{8}$.

# 5 *New worlds*

## 5.4 Metric spaces

> (a) Is the point, labelled *P*, also 5 units away from *A*?
>
> (b) Are all the points on the lines 5 units from *A*?

(a) and (b)

It can be argued that, in Taxicab geometry, only the grid intersection points have any meaning. If this view is **not** taken, then *P* and the other points on the lines would be 5 units from *A*.

# COMMENTARIES

# *Equations of circles*

CIRCLES

COMMENTARY

TASKSHEET 1

**1** (a) (i) $CT = x - 8$

(ii) $PT = y - 6$

(b) $CTP$ is a right-angled triangle, so, by Pythagoras' Theorem

$$CT^2 + PT^2 = 5^2$$

(c) $(x - 8)^2 + (y - 6)^2 = 25$

**2** (a) $x^2 + y^2 = 9$

(b) $(x - 8)^2 + (y - 6)^2 = 9$

(c) $\begin{bmatrix} 8 \\ 6 \end{bmatrix}$

**3** (a) $\begin{bmatrix} a \\ b \end{bmatrix}$

(b) $(x - a)^2 + (y - b)^2 = r^2$

# *Tutorial sheet*

**1**   (a)

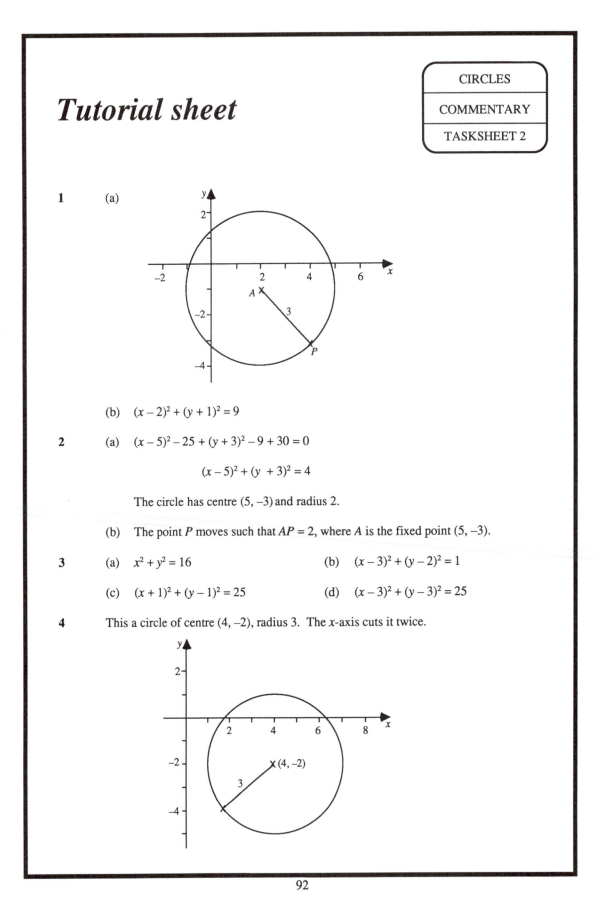

(b)   $(x - 2)^2 + (y + 1)^2 = 9$

**2**   (a)   $(x - 5)^2 - 25 + (y + 3)^2 - 9 + 30 = 0$

$$(x - 5)^2 + (y + 3)^2 = 4$$

The circle has centre $(5, -3)$ and radius 2.

(b)   The point $P$ moves such that $AP = 2$, where $A$ is the fixed point $(5, -3)$.

**3**   (a)   $x^2 + y^2 = 16$          (b)   $(x - 3)^2 + (y - 2)^2 = 1$

(c)   $(x + 1)^2 + (y - 1)^2 = 25$          (d)   $(x - 3)^2 + (y - 3)^2 = 25$

**4**   This a circle of centre $(4, -2)$, radius 3.  The $x$-axis cuts it twice.

# *The perpendicular bisector*

**1**    $AP = PB$ for any point $P$ on the locus.  In particular, $AP_1 = P_1B$ and so the triangle $AP_1B$ is isosceles.

**2**

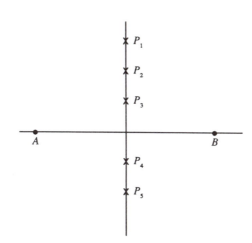

**3 and 4**  The locus is a straight line.  This line is **perpendicular** to the line $AB$ and passes through the **midpoint** of $AB$ (i.e. it **bisects** line $AB$).  It is called the **perpendicular bisector** of $AB$.

**5**    The locus is always the perpendicular bisector of $AB$.

**6**    If $A$ and $B$ were the same point, then **all** points would be equidistant from $A$ and $B$!

# *For any ratio*

**1**     (a),(b)   The locus appears to be a circle, centre (6, 0), radius 4 units.

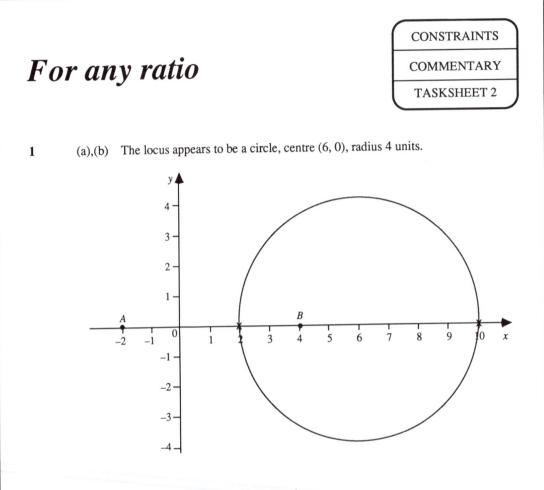

**2**     The circle moves to the right and becomes larger.

**3**     The locus is now a circle, centre (–4, 0) radius 4 units.

**4**     If $\lambda = 1$, the locus is the perpendicular bisector of *AB*.

If $\lambda > 1$, a circle containing *B* is obtained.

If $\lambda < 1$, the circle contains *A*.

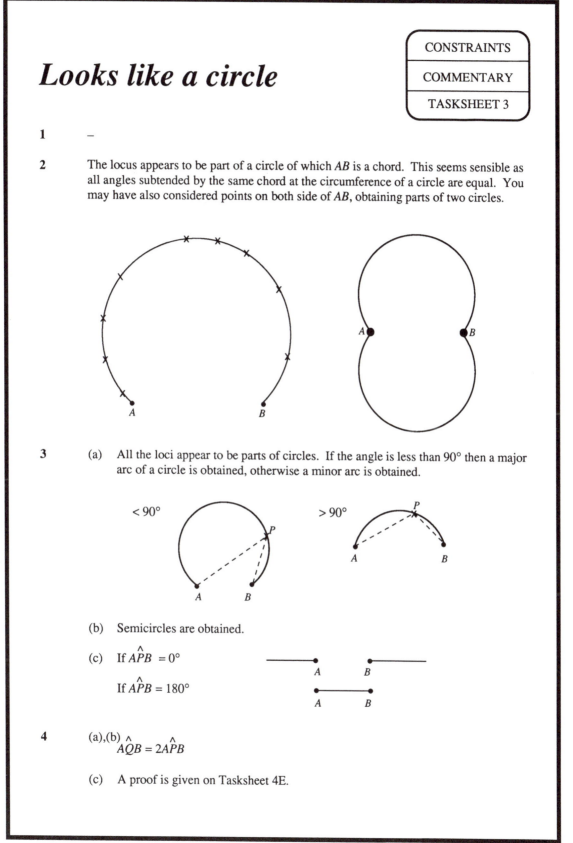

# *Looks like a circle*

**1**    –

**2**    The locus appears to be part of a circle of which *AB* is a chord. This seems sensible as all angles subtended by the same chord at the circumference of a circle are equal. You may have also considered points on both side of *AB*, obtaining parts of two circles.

**3**    (a)    All the loci appear to be parts of circles. If the angle is less than 90° then a major arc of a circle is obtained, otherwise a minor arc is obtained.

&lt; 90°     &gt; 90°

(b)    Semicircles are obtained.

(c)    If $A\hat{P}B = 0°$

If $A\hat{P}B = 180°$

**4**    (a),(b) $A\hat{Q}B = 2A\hat{P}B$

(c)    A proof is given on Tasksheet 4E.

95

# *The proof*

**1** Triangle $ACQ$ is isoceles, with $AC = CQ$

So $A\hat{C}Q = 180 - C\hat{A}Q - C\hat{Q}A$

$\qquad = 180 - 2a$

**2** $A\hat{C}Q$, $Q\hat{C}B$ and $2\theta$ are the angles at the point $C$ and so sum to $360°$.

Therefore $(180 - 2a) + (180 - 2b) + 2\theta = 360$

$\qquad \Rightarrow \quad 360 - 2a - 2b + 2\theta = 360$

$\qquad \Rightarrow \qquad 2\theta = 2a + 2b$

$\qquad \Rightarrow \qquad \theta = a + b$

**3** $A\hat{Q}B = A\hat{Q}C + C\hat{Q}B$

$\qquad = a + b$

$\qquad = \theta$, from ④.

**4** $P$ was defined as the point on line $AP$ such that $APB = \theta$, so $Q$ must be $P$.

**5** $2\theta$ is drawn as the angle in a triangle and so $0° < 2\theta < 180° \Rightarrow 0° < \theta < 90°$.

**6**

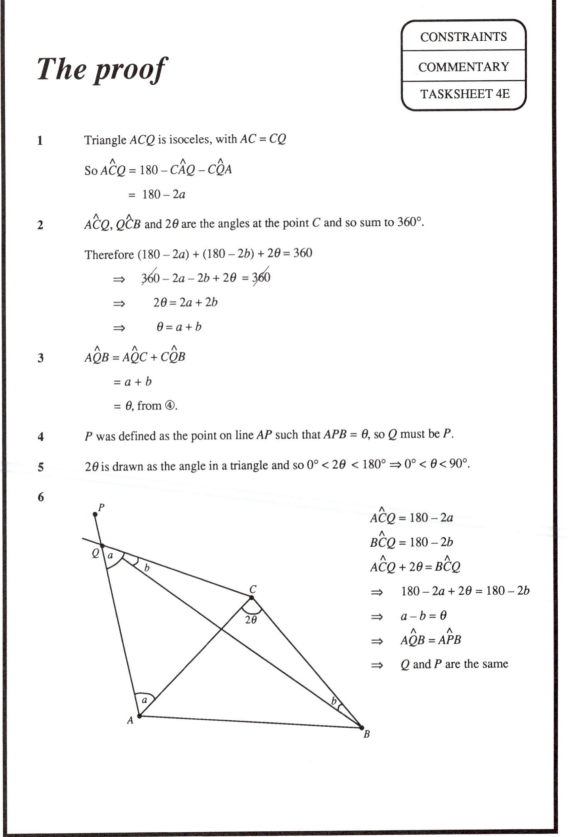

$A\hat{C}Q = 180 - 2a$

$B\hat{C}Q = 180 - 2b$

$A\hat{C}Q + 2\theta = B\hat{C}Q$

$\qquad \Rightarrow \quad 180 - 2a + 2\theta = 180 - 2b$

$\qquad \Rightarrow \qquad a - b = \theta$

$\qquad \Rightarrow \qquad A\hat{Q}B = A\hat{P}B$

$\qquad \Rightarrow \qquad Q$ and $P$ are the same

# Tutorial sheet

**1** (a) $0 = \lambda$      The point $A$.
         $0 < \lambda < 1$      A circle enclosing $A$.
         $1 = \lambda$      The perpendicular bisector of $AB$.
         $1 < \lambda < 2$      A circle enclosing $B$.

(b)

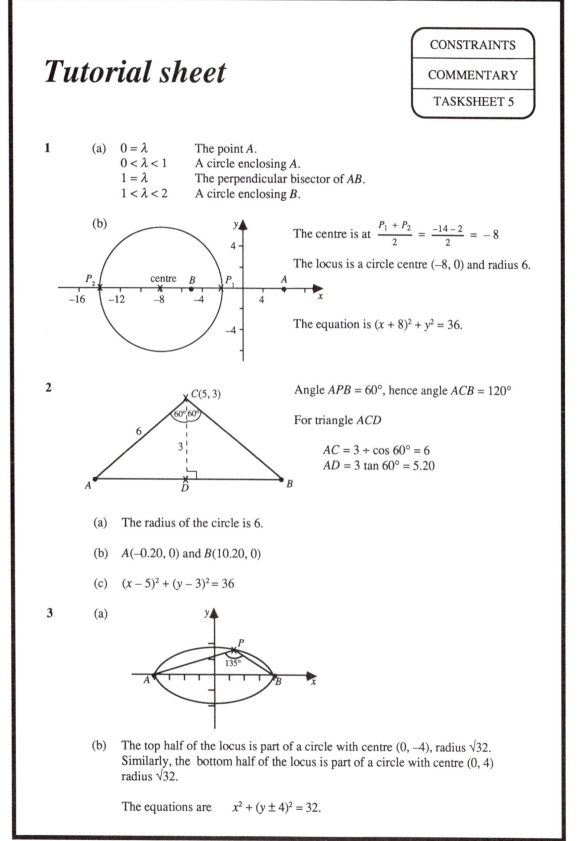

The centre is at $\dfrac{P_1 + P_2}{2} = \dfrac{-14 - 2}{2} = -8$

The locus is a circle centre $(-8, 0)$ and radius 6.

The equation is $(x + 8)^2 + y^2 = 36$.

**2**

Angle $APB = 60°$, hence angle $ACB = 120°$

For triangle $ACD$

$$AC = 3 \div \cos 60° = 6$$
$$AD = 3 \tan 60° = 5.20$$

(a) The radius of the circle is 6.

(b) $A(-0.20, 0)$ and $B(10.20, 0)$

(c) $(x - 5)^2 + (y - 3)^2 = 36$

**3** (a)

(b) The top half of the locus is part of a circle with centre $(0, -4)$, radius $\sqrt{32}$. Similarly, the bottom half of the locus is part of a circle with centre $(0, 4)$ radius $\sqrt{32}$.

The equations are     $x^2 + (y \pm 4)^2 = 32$.

# *Imagination or reality?*

**1**   (a)   The conic section or cut that will be made is a closed curve and is called
an ellipse.

(b)   The sketch should resemble a stretched circle and have two lines of symmetry.

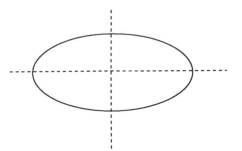

**2**   Looking sideways at a cone labelled
*ABC*, *D* and *E* are two points on a
horizontal cut. *D* and *G* are two
points on a cut made parallel to the
edge *AB*.

Any cut made between *DE* and *DG*,
such as *DF*, will give an elliptical
conic section (see question 1 above).

When the cut is between *DB* and *DG*,
the section will be part of an ellipse.

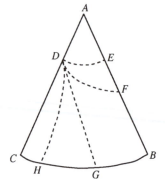

(a), (b)   The cut *DG* will give a parabolic conic section. This curve is not closed and
has a line of symmetry through its vertex at *D*.

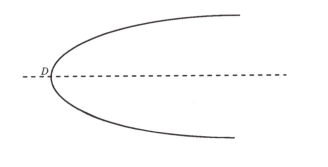

(continued)

Any cut made between *DG* and *DC*, such as *DH*, will give a hyperbolic conic section. This curve is usually shown as having two parts which can be obtained by cutting two cones placed vertex to vertex.

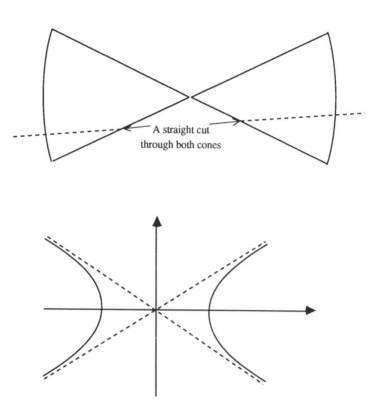

The hyperbola has two lines of symmetry and a pair of asymptotes.

Any cut made through *A* perpendicular to the base of the cone will give a triangle. This is a special case of the hyperbola.

# *Changing the ratio*

1 (a) $AP_1 = 2$, $P_1B = 4$, so $\dfrac{AP_1}{P_1B} = \dfrac{1}{2}$

$AP_2 = 6$, $P_2B = 12$, so $\dfrac{AP_2}{P_2B} = \dfrac{1}{2}$

(b)

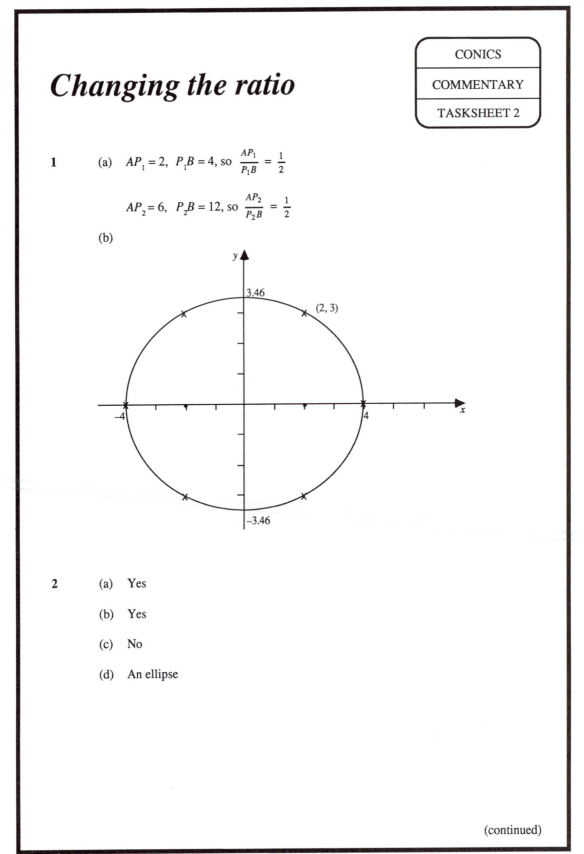

2 (a) Yes

(b) Yes

(c) No

(d) An ellipse

(continued)

**3**      A parabola

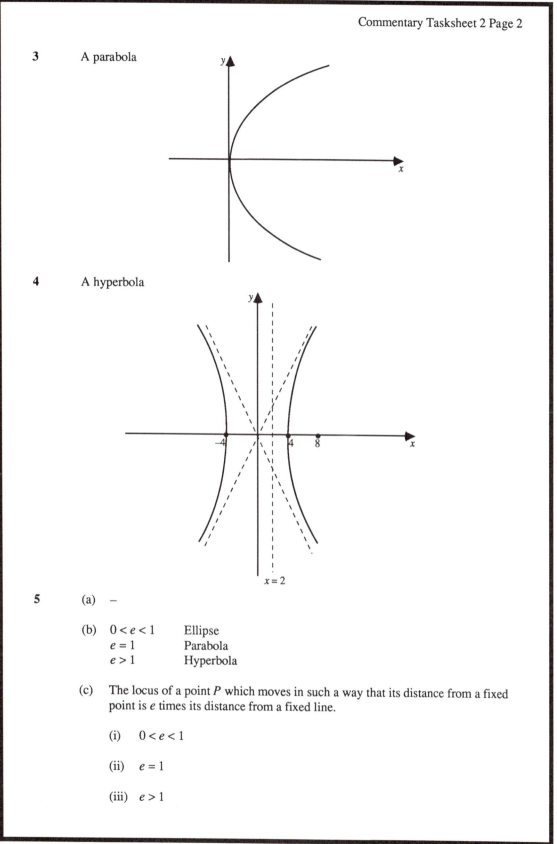

**4**      A hyperbola

**5**      (a)    –

   (b)   $0 < e < 1$         Ellipse
         $e = 1$            Parabola
         $e > 1$            Hyperbola

   (c)   The locus of a point $P$ which moves in such a way that its distance from a fixed
         point is $e$ times its distance from a fixed line.

         (i)     $0 < e < 1$

         (ii)    $e = 1$

         (iii)   $e > 1$

# *Sums and differences*

**1**     (a)    (iv)    $AP_i = 6, BP_i = 10 \Rightarrow AP_i + BP_i = 16$, as required.

        (b)

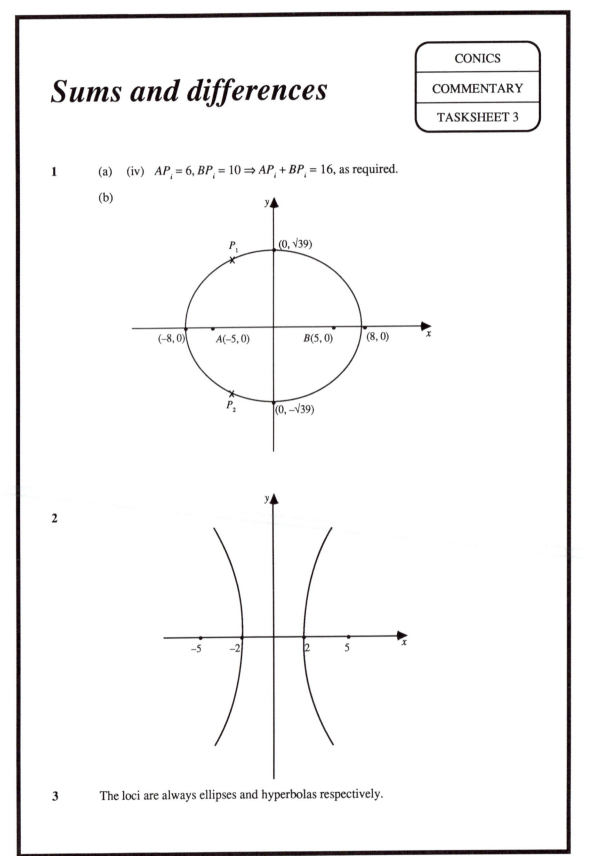

**2**

**3**      The loci are always ellipses and hyperbolas respectively.

# *Tutorial sheet*

**1**  (a)  $SA = 1, AN = \frac{13}{12} \Rightarrow \frac{SA}{AN} = \frac{12}{13}$

  (b)  $A$ is one of the points $P_i$ on the locus, hence $e = \frac{12}{13}$ .

  The point $P$ moves such that the distance from the point $S(12, 0)$ to $P$ is $\frac{12}{13}$ of the distance from $P$ to the line $x = \frac{169}{12}$ .

**2**  (a)  $SA = 12, AN = 4 \Rightarrow \frac{SA}{AN} = 3$

  (b)  $A$ is one of the points $P_i$ on the locus hence $e = 3$.

  The point $P$ moves such that the distance from $P$ to the point $S(18, 0)$ is three times the distance from $P$ to the line $x = 2$.

**3**  (a)  $SA = 1, S'A = 49 \Rightarrow SA + S'A = 50$

  (b)  $A$ is one the points $P_i$ on the locus hence $SP + S'P = 50$ for all points $P$.

  The point $P$ moves such that, for two fixed points $S(24, 0)$ and $S'(-24, 0)$, $SP + S'P = 50$.

# *Parameters*

**1**         $y = 6t \Rightarrow t = \frac{y}{6}$

      $\Rightarrow$    $x = 3 \left( \frac{y}{6} \right)^2$

      $\Rightarrow$    $12x = y^2$

**2**     (a)      $x^2 = 4a^2t^2$

            $\Rightarrow$    $x^2 = 4ay$

    (b)   This curve is also a parabola but its axis is along the $y$-axis.

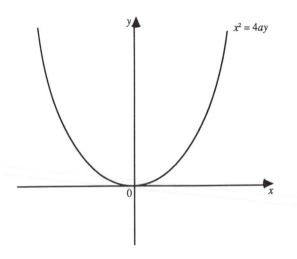

      Its vertex is at the origin.

# *a and b*

**1**  (a)   $y^2 = 16 \left(1 - \dfrac{x^2}{9}\right)$

so  $y = \pm 4 \sqrt{\left(1 - \dfrac{x^2}{9}\right)}$

(b), (c)

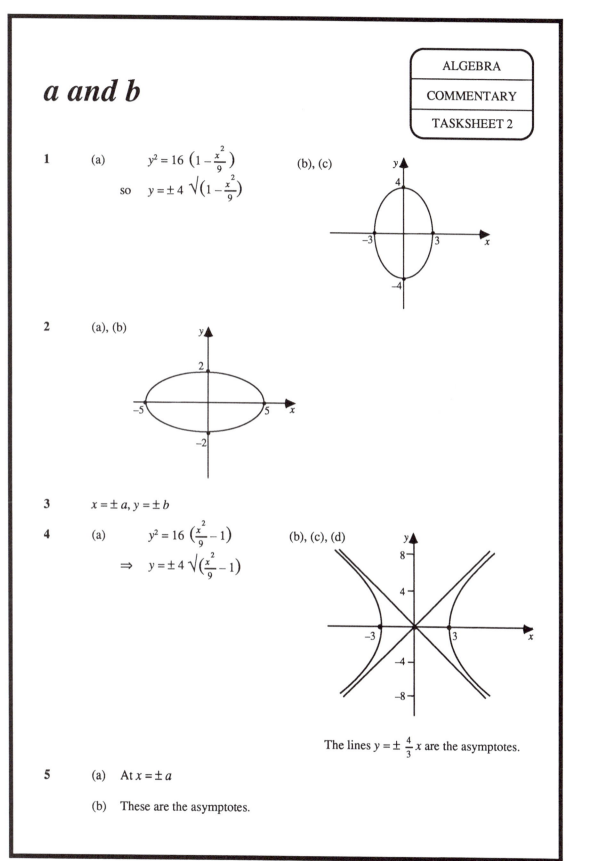

**2**  (a), (b)

**3**  $x = \pm a,\ y = \pm b$

**4**  (a)   $y^2 = 16 \left(\dfrac{x^2}{9} - 1\right)$

$\Rightarrow\ \ y = \pm 4 \sqrt{\left(\dfrac{x^2}{9} - 1\right)}$

(b), (c), (d)

The lines $y = \pm \dfrac{4}{3} x$ are the asymptotes.

**5**  (a)   At $x = \pm a$

(b)   These are the asymptotes.

# *Facts and formulas*

1    The distances from $A$ to $S$ and $S'$ are $a - s$ and $a + s$, respectively. Equation ① represents the fact that the sum of these distances is $2a$.

By symmetry, $S'B = SB$ (equation ②) and so equation ③ follows from the fact that the sum of these distances is $2a$.

The definition of eccentricity is $SP = ePN$. Equations ④ and ⑤ are this result for $P$ at $B$ and $A'$, respectively.

By Pythagoras, $OB^2 + OS^2 = BS^2$ and so $b^2 + s^2 = a^2$ (equation ⑥).

2    (a)    Squaring both sides of ⑦,

$$(x - s)^2 + y^2 = e^2(n - x)^2$$

$$x^2 - 2xs + s^2 + y^2 = e^2n^2 - 2e^2nx + e^2x^2$$

$$x^2(1 - e^2) + 2x(ne^2 - s) + y^2 = e^2n^2 - s^2$$

(b)    (i)    $b^2 = a^2(1 - e)^2$ was obtained from ⑥ and so $1 - e^2 = \dfrac{b^2}{a^2}$.

(ii)    $a = en$ and $s = ae$ were obtained from ④ and ⑤ respectively.

Therefore $s = (en)e = e^2n$ and so $ne^2 - s = 0$.

(iii)    From ⑥, $b^2 + s^2 = a^2 = e^2n^2$

$$\Rightarrow e^2n^2 - s^2 = b^2$$

(c)    Equation ⑧ then becomes

$$x^2\,\frac{b^2}{a^2} + 2x \times 0 + y^2 = b^2$$

$$\Rightarrow \frac{x^2}{a^2} + \frac{y^2}{b^2} = 1$$

# *Parametric form*

**1**     The general equation of an ellipse, centred on the origin and with axes along the coordinate axes is of the form

$$\frac{x^2}{a^2} + \frac{y^2}{b^2} = 1$$

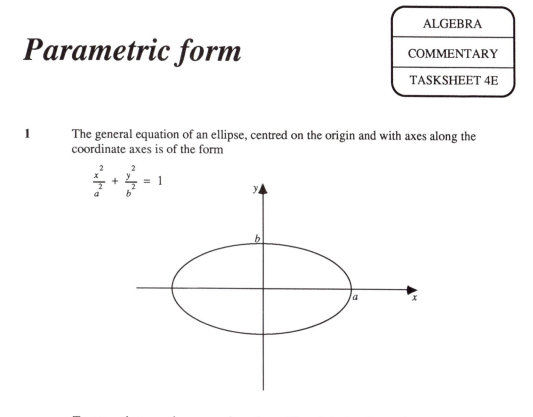

To prove that any given curve is such an ellipse, it is therefore only necesary to show that its equation can be put into this form.

**2**     Line ① is $\cos^2\theta + \sin^2\theta$.

Consider the right-angled triangle shown.

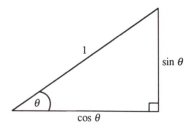

By Pythagoras,

$\cos^2\theta + \sin^2\theta = 1$, as required.

# *Asymptotes*

**1**     The hyperbola is symmetrical under reflection in the *x*-axis (replacing *x* by –*x*) and also under reflection in the *y*-axis (replacing *y* by – *y*).  Any asymptotes must also be symmetric under these reflections.

**2**     (a)     $\dfrac{y^2}{16} = \dfrac{x^2}{25} - 1$

$y^2 = \dfrac{16}{25}(x^2 - 25)$

$y = \pm \dfrac{4}{5}\sqrt{(x^2 - 25)}$

(b)     As *x* becomes very large, $\sqrt{(x^2 - 25)}$ becomes indistinguishable from *x* and so the curve looks like $y = \pm \dfrac{4}{5}x$.

**3**     $y = \pm \dfrac{b}{a}x$

**4**     (a)     A translation by $\begin{bmatrix} c \\ d \end{bmatrix}$

(b)     Translating $y = \pm \dfrac{b}{a}x$ by the same vector gives

$y - d = \pm \dfrac{b}{a}(x - c).$

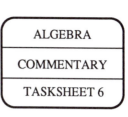
1  (a)  $y^2 = 4ax \Rightarrow 4a = 64 \Rightarrow a = 16$.

(b)  The point $P$ moves such that the distance from the point $S(16, 0)$ to $P$ equals the distance from $P$ to the line $x = -16$.

2  (a)  $a = \sqrt{169} = 13, \ b = \sqrt{25} = 5, \ b^2 = a^2(1 - e^2)$

$$\Rightarrow \frac{25}{169} = 1 - e^2 \Rightarrow e^2 = 1 - \frac{25}{169} = \frac{144}{169} \Rightarrow e = \frac{12}{13}$$

$$n = \frac{a}{e} = \frac{169}{12}, \ s = ae = 12$$

(b)  The point $P$ moves such that the distance from the point $S(12, 0)$ to $P$ is $\frac{12}{13}$ of the distance from $P$ to the line $x = \frac{169}{12}$.

(c)  $l = 2a \Rightarrow l = 26$

The point $P$ moves such that, for two fixed points $S(12, 0)$ and $S'(-12, 0)$, $SP + S'P = 26$.

3  (a)  $a = \sqrt{4} = 2, \ b = \sqrt{9} = 3, \ b^2 = a^2(e^2 - 1)$

$$\Rightarrow \frac{9}{4} = e^2 - 1 \Rightarrow e^2 = \frac{13}{4} \Rightarrow e = \frac{\sqrt{13}}{2}$$

$$n = \frac{a}{e} = \frac{4}{\sqrt{13}}, \ s = ae = \sqrt{13}$$

(b)  The point $P$ moves such that the distance from the point $S(\sqrt{13}, 0)$ to $P$ is $\frac{\sqrt{13}}{2}$ times the distance from $P$ to the line $x = \frac{4}{\sqrt{13}}$.

(c)  $SA = \sqrt{13} - 2, \ S'A = \sqrt{13} + 2, \ |SA - S'A| = 4$

The point $P$ moves such that, for two fixed points $S(\sqrt{13}, 0)$ and $S'(-\sqrt{13}, 0)$, $|SP - S'P| = 4$.

# *Falling ladders*

**1**     The point $P_4$ is the midpoint of the ladder when it is lying horizontally.

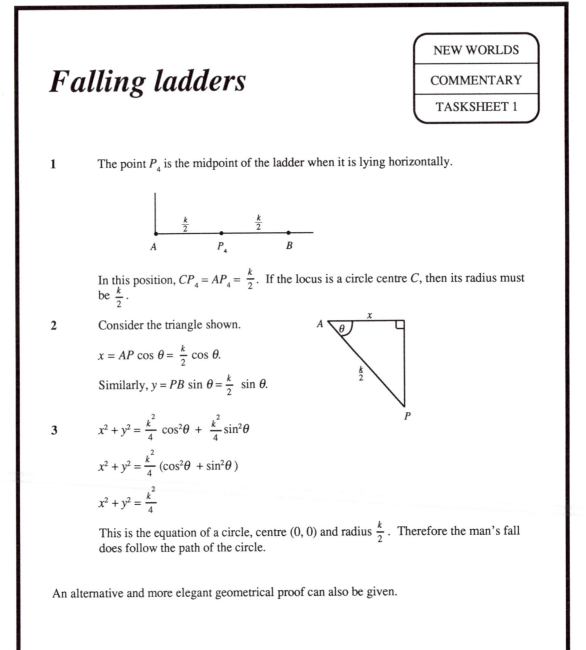

In this position, $CP_4 = AP_4 = \frac{k}{2}$. If the locus is a circle centre $C$, then its radius must be $\frac{k}{2}$.

**2**     Consider the triangle shown.

$x = AP \cos \theta = \frac{k}{2} \cos \theta.$

Similarly, $y = PB \sin \theta = \frac{k}{2} \sin \theta.$

**3**     $x^2 + y^2 = \frac{k^2}{4} \cos^2\theta + \frac{k^2}{4} \sin^2\theta$

$x^2 + y^2 = \frac{k^2}{4} (\cos^2\theta + \sin^2\theta)$

$x^2 + y^2 = \frac{k^2}{4}$

This is the equation of a circle, centre $(0, 0)$ and radius $\frac{k}{2}$. Therefore the man's fall does follow the path of the circle.

An alternative and more elegant geometrical proof can also be given.

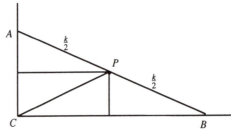

All four small triangles in the diagram can be easily shown to be congruent.

$CP$ is therefore $\frac{k}{2}$, for **any** position of the ladder.

# *The Octopus*

**1**

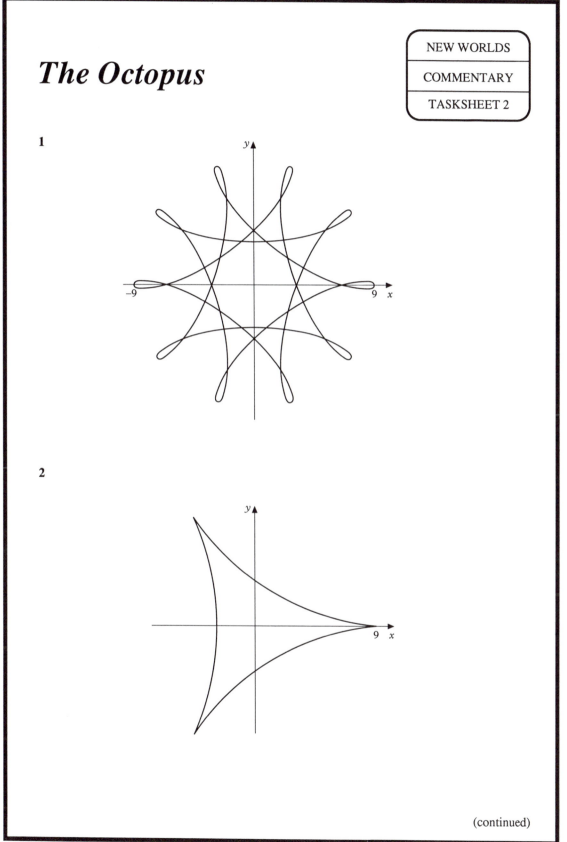

**2**

(continued)

111

**3**

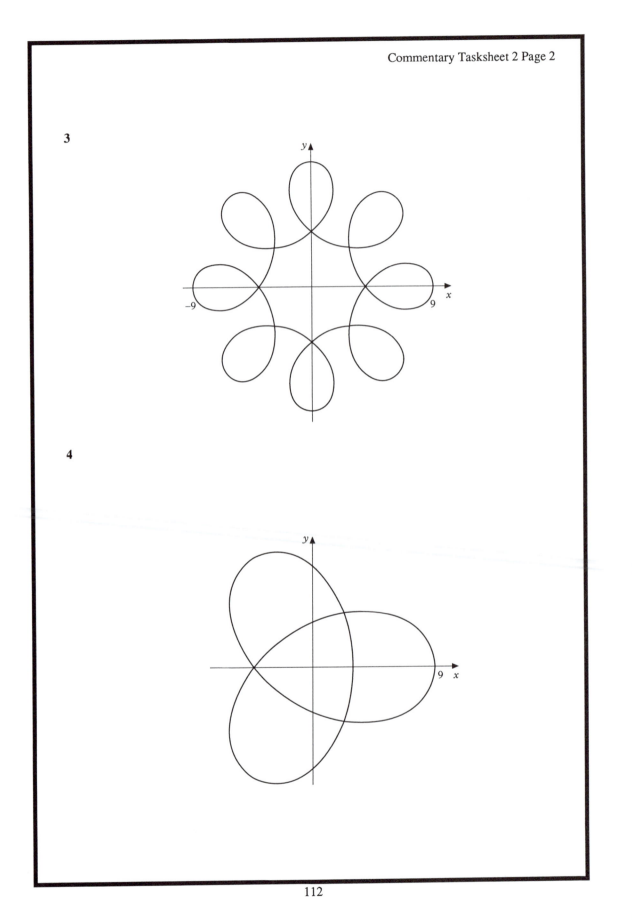

**4**

# *Apollonius' circles*

**1**

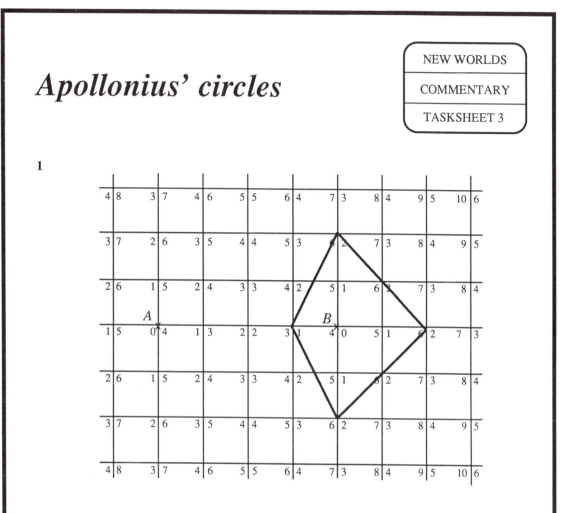

| | | | | | | | | | | | |
|---|---|---|---|---|---|---|---|---|---|---|---|
| 4 8 | 3 7 | 4 6 | 5 5 | 6 4 | 7 3 | 8 4 | 9 5 | 10 6 |
| 3 7 | 2 6 | 3 5 | 4 4 | 5 3 | 6 2 | 7 3 | 8 4 | 9 5 |
| 2 6 | 1 5 | 2 4 | 3 3 | 4 2 | 5 1 | 6 2 | 7 3 | 8 4 |
| 1 5 | 0 4 | 1 3 | 2 2 | 3 1 | 4 0 | 5 1 | 6 2 | 7 3 |
| 2 6 | 1 5 | 2 4 | 3 3 | 4 2 | 5 1 | 6 2 | 7 3 | 8 4 |
| 3 7 | 2 6 | 3 5 | 4 4 | 5 3 | 6 2 | 7 3 | 8 4 | 9 5 |
| 4 8 | 3 7 | 4 6 | 5 5 | 6 4 | 7 3 | 8 4 | 9 5 | 10 6 |

**2**   In Euclidean geometry this gives a circle but here the result is not a Taxicab circle. It has horizontal symmetry but there is no vertical line of symmetry.

The lack of symmetry is a clue that, in Taxicab geometry, the shape of the locus depends upon the direction of the line *AB*.

113

# DATASHEET

# Fixed angle loci

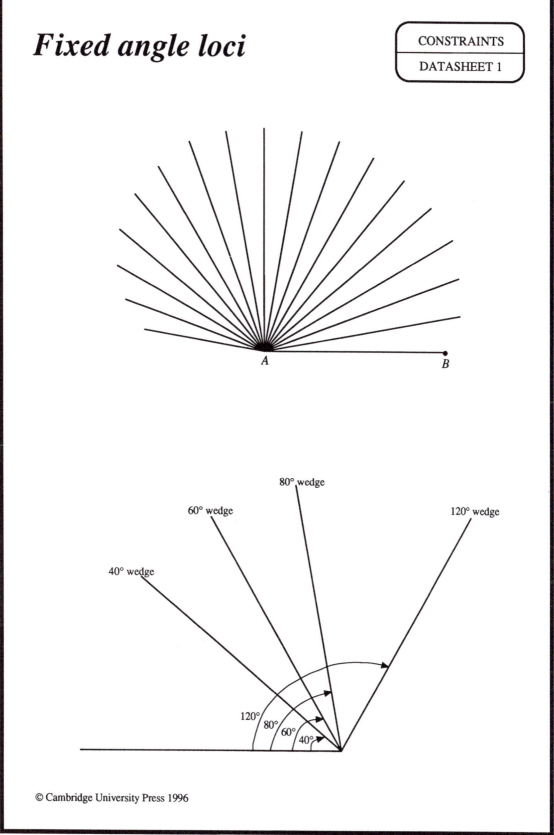

40° wedge

60° wedge

80° wedge

120° wedge

120°

80°

60°

40°